The McMurtrys' first cabin in Archer County

LARRY MCMURTRY

WALTER BENJAMIN
AT THE
DAIRY QUEEN

*Reflections at Sixty
and Beyond*

SIMON & SCHUSTER

Simon & Schuster
Rockefeller Center
1230 Avenue of the Americas
New York, NY 10020
Copyright © 1999 by Larry McMurtry

Designed by Karolina Harris
Manufactured in the United States of America
10 9 8 7 6 5 4 3 2
Library of Congress Cataloging-in-Publication Data
McMurtry, Larry.
Walter Benjamin at the Dairy Queen :
reflections at sixty and beyond / Larry McMurtry
p.   cm.
1. McMurtry, Larry. 2. McMurtry, Larry—Books and reading. 3. McMurtry,
Larry—Homes and haunts—Texas. 4. Novelists, American—20th century—Biography. 5. Antiquarian booksellers—United States—Biography.
6. Books and reading—Texas. 7. Texas—Biography. I. Title.
PS3563.A319Z475   1999   99-19346   CIP
813'.54—dc21
[b]
ISBN 0-684-85496-1

For James, Elena, Curtis

Boredom is the dream bird that hatches
the egg of experience.

WALTER BENJAMIN

Modern man no longer works at that
which cannot be abbreviated.

PAUL VALÉRY

PLACE—AND THE MEMORIES OF PLACE

1

◌ IN THE summer of 1980, in the Archer City Dairy Queen, while nursing a lime Dr Pepper (a delicacy strictly local, unheard of even in the next Dairy Queen down the road—Olney's, eighteen miles south—but easily obtainable by anyone willing to buy a lime and a Dr Pepper), I opened a book called *Illuminations* and read Walter Benjamin's essay "The Storyteller," nominally a study of or reflection on the stories of Nikolay Leskov, but really (I came to feel, after several rereadings) an examination, and a profound one, of the growing obsolescence of what might be called practical memory and the consequent diminution of the power of oral narrative in our twentieth-century lives.

The place where I first read the essay, Archer City's Dairy Queen, was apposite in more ways than one. Dairy Queens, simple drive-up eateries, taverns without alcohol, began to appear in the arid little towns of west Texas about the same time (the late sixties) that Walter Benjamin's work began to arrive in the English language—in the case of *Illuminations,* beautifully introduced by Hannah Arendt. The aridity of the small west Texas towns was not all a matter of unforgiving skies, baking heat, and rainlessness, either; the drought in those towns was social, as well as climatic. The extent to which it was moral is a question we can table for the moment. What I remember clearly is that before the Dairy Queens appeared the people of the small towns had no place to meet and talk; and so they didn't meet *or* talk, which meant that much local lore or incident remained private and ceased to be exchanged, debated, and stored as local lore had been during the centuries that Benjamin describes.

The Dairy Queens, by providing a comfortable setting that made possible hundreds of small, informal local forums, revived, for a time, the potential for storytelling of the sort Walter Benjamin favored. Whether what he favored actually occurred, as opposed to remaining potential, is a question I want to consider in this essay.

On that morning in 1980, Benjamin's tremendous elegy to the storyteller as a figure of critical importance in the human community prompted me to look around the room, at that hour of the morning lightly peopled with scattered groups of coffee drinkers, to see whether I could spot a loquacious villager who—even at that late cultural hour—might be telling a story. And if so, was anyone really listening?

Certainly if there were places in west Texas where stories might sometimes be told, those places would be the local Dairy Queens: clean, well-lighted places open commonly from 6 A.M. until ten at night. These Dairy Queens combined the functions of tavern, café, and general store; they were simple local roadhouses where both rambling men and stay-at-homes could meet. To them would come men of all crafts and women of all dispositions. The oilmen would be there at six in the morning; the courthouse crowd would show up about ten; cowboys would stop for lunch or a midafternoon respite; roughnecks would jump out of their trucks or pickups to snatch a cheeseburger as their schedules allowed; and the women of the villages might appear at any time, often merely to sit and mingle for a few minutes; they might smoke, sip,

14

touch themselves up, have a cup of coffee or a glass of iced tea, sample the gossip of the moment, and leave. Regular attendance was necessary if one hoped to hear the freshest gossip, which soon went stale. Most local scandals were flogged to death within a day or two; only the steamiest goings-on could hold the community's attention for as long as a week.

And always, there were diners who were just passing through, few of whom aspired to stay in Archer City. They stopped at the Dairy Queen as they would at a gas station, to pee and take in fuel, mindful, gloomily, that it was still a good hundred miles even to Abilene, itself no isle of grace. Few of these nomads, if they had stories to tell, bothered to tell them to the locals—and if they *had* wanted to tell a story or two, it is doubtful that anyone would have listened. People on their way to Abilene might as well be on their way to hell—why talk to them? Folks in Archer City knew the way to hell well enough; they need seek no guidance from traveling men.

ALL DAY the little groups in the Dairy Queen formed and re-formed, like drifting clouds. I stayed put, imbibed a few more lime Dr Peppers, and reread "The Storyteller," concluding that Walter Benjamin was undoubtedly right. Storytellers were nearly extinct, like whooping cranes, but the D.Q. was at least the right tide pool in which to observe the few that remained.

"The Storyteller" had been published in a journal called *Orient und Okzident* in the year of my birth (1936, well before electricity had arrived in the rural parts of the county where I grew up; it arrived, dramatically, when I was five, courtesy, we all felt, of FDR). It was startling to sit in that Dairy Queen, reading the words of a cosmopolitan European, a man of Berlin, Moscow, Paris, and realize that what he was describing with a clear sad eye was more or less exactly what had happened in my own small dusty county in my lifetime. I was born, in the year of the essay, into a world of rural storytellers—and what had become of them? Were any of the coffee drinkers sitting nearby doing any more than escaping the heat? Were they exchanging experiences, were they curious about life, or were they just hot?

If the latter, they could hardly be blamed—the temperature had soared to a Sudan-like 116 that day, forcing the cancellation of the long-awaited (a century awaited), first ever Archer County marathon, a much anticipated high spot of the county's centennial celebration, itself a fortnight-long event, or congeries of events, which I had come home to watch. The celebration was certainly appropriate, but the marathon was a different matter, one in which I personally had not been able to invest much belief. Though I had long made a living by imagining unlikely lives, it was nonetheless not easy to imagine the county's dairy farmers and roughnecks and cowboys, and their wives or women, lumbering along the county's roads for anything like twenty-six miles. The marathoners, if any, would undoubtedly be imports, pros or semipros whose connection to our one-hundred-year-old county would very likely be negligible. All the same, calling off the run on a day when it was going to be 116 seemed a wise, even a compassionate policy. At 116 Fahrenheit people are likely to drop dead while doing nothing more strenuous than picking their teeth.

2

◻ "IN EVERY case the storyteller is a man who has counsel for his readers. But if today 'having counsel' is beginning to have an old fashioned ring to it it is because the communicability of experience is decreasing," says Walter Benjamin.

One reason he offers in explaining why we no longer exchange experience (by telling or listening to stories) is that experience has fallen in value—"and it looks as if it will continue to fall into bottomlessness," he adds, blaming the First World War for having made human moral experience, as it had been up to 1914, meaningless. His point, whether one agrees with it or not, is a corollary to Virginia Woolf's famous remark that in or about December 1910 human nature changed, in part, it seems, because Lytton Strachey said the word "semen" at a party.

How much human nature changed, or how much meaning or value human experience lost, depended, in a measure, upon where you were at the time. Archer County had been an organized unit of civilization for only thirty-two years in 1912, and my paternal grandparents had been settled in it for most of that time. They were of course not aware of Strachey's comment, or Virginia Woolf's remark, or Roger Fry's startling Postimpressionist exhibitions, or even of the looming war that would soon split the earth and sunder populous societies. The war that still loomed prominently in the consciousness of frontier citizens such as my grandparents was the long guerrilla war that had been concluded, more or less, in the mid-1870s, when the power of the Comanches and the Kiowas was finally broken. My grandparents, like many prudent frontier citizens, lingered in safety about one hundred miles short of their eventual destination while these bloody hostilities wound down. It was *that* war that had kept Archer County largely unsettled and unsurveyed for so long, while other, safer counties were filling up. The settlers stayed back, waiting, hesitating, wondering whether the empty, farmable, homesteadable *Comancheria* was finally safe—or at least relatively so. Until well past the end of the nineteenth century the attention of pioneers along that particular stretch of Texas frontier was still focused north, whence the terrible raiding parties had come for so long: north beyond the Canadian, north even beyond the Arkansas. These settlers had no attention to spare, just then, for Europe—the Europe of Benjamin, Proust, Rilke, the Woolfs, Lloyd George, the Kaiser, the Czar, Balfour, Lenin. Their heroes were still mainly the heroes of the Confederacy, Jackson and Lee, their demons not anarchists or communists but Sherman, Sheridan, Grant—the men, as they saw it, who had defeated the South.

And what, I wonder, would contemplation of the emptiness, geographical and social, that my grandparents faced when they came to Archer County have suggested to Walter Benjamin? They came to nowhere and nothing at about the time that Benjamin's well-to-do parents were moving to an even more affluent, more upscale Berlin suburb. His reflections on the storyteller, though meant to describe a universal figure, were still drawn from the dense context of European life. What experiences would he have expected to hear exchanged in Archer County, in those first years?

3

☐ MY OWN experience, growing up in the county about fifty years after it was settled, was that in the female, at least, what frontier experience produced was silence. In two cases in particular it seemed to have produced absolute silence.

In a tent (later a shack) not far south of our ranch house, in post oak scrub near the West Fork of the Trinity River, lived a woman who had (reportedly) been traded for a whole winter's catch of skunk hides, the exchange occurring when she was about thirteen. The man who had her (by what right I don't know) stopped to spend the night in the camp of a skunk trapper, who immediately took a fancy to the girl—such a fancy, indeed, that he offered his winter's catch for her. The traveler took the hides and left the girl, who lived to bear the trapper many children; she stayed down near West Fork for the rest of her life. When, as an old woman, she would occasionally need to go to town for some reason, she simply walked out to the nearest dirt road and stood, in silence, until some passerby picked her up and took her where she was going. This passerby was often my father, though sometimes it was the school bus I rode in. I rode to town with the old woman—once worth more than fifty skunk hides—many times but I never heard her speak a single word. She was through with talk, one thing she had in common with

Louisa Francis McMurtry, my paternal grandmother, who was also through with talk, at least conditionally. Now and then I heard my grandmother talking to my father—her favorite of twelve children—but although she lived with us until her death (when I was eight), I cannot recall her ever addressing a single syllable to me. Her silence had a quality of implacability which I have never forgotten—it made me want to go live in the barn. But Louisa Francis had raised twelve children on a stark frontier, with a husband who was at times erratic (that is, drunk); by the time I came along her interest in children was understandably slight—and that's putting it mildly. Older cousins remember her as lively; I just remember her as scary. Whatever stories she and the old skunk woman had were not of the sort to be shared with little boys.

4

☐ MY PATERNAL grandfather, William Jefferson McMurtry, an American Scot with a fine mustache and an inquisitive mind, liked to whittle his own toothpicks. He favored cedarwood, both for its whittling qualities and for its sweet smell, but in a pinch, he would take out his pocketknife and whittle a toothpick from any wood available—a plank on the outhouse even, if he happened to be standing near it. (When I was three a great white snow owl flew out of that outhouse, right in my face, a thing so frightening that I have never fully recovered from the scare.) The decline of whittling, which is the slow paring away of a stick, usually for no purpose other than to occupy the hands, has clearly deprived storytellers of many willing listeners—most of the old men who filled the spit-and-whittle benches outside the rural courthouses of my youth regaled themselves as they whittled with story after story, the residue, in most cases, of their own somewhat splotchy memories or the memories of their kin.

My grandparents were—potent word—*pioneers*. They came to an unsettled place, a prairie emptiness, a place where no past was—no Anglo-Saxon past, at least, and not even much Native American past. Comanches, Kiowas, Kickapoos, and other tribal nomads had passed over and no doubt occasionally camped on the low hill where my grandparents stopped their wagon and made their home place; the nomads, like my grandparents, probably stopped there because a fine seeping spring assured them of plentiful water. But the Comanches and the Kiowas were only passing through, on their way to raid the ever more populous settlements to the southeast. They were a brilliantly militant people—the burn they left on the psyches of the first Texas settlers had only now faded out. The more placid Kickapoos were never very numerous and did not impress themselves much either on the land or on history.

If I repeat the fact of an initial emptiness, and emphasize it throughout this essay, it is because it is so important to my own effort at self-understanding. I spent every day of my young life with William Jefferson and Louisa Francis McMurtry and, consequently, am one of the few writers who can still claim to have had prolonged and intimate contact with first-generation American pioneers, men and women who came to a nearly absolute emptiness and began the filling of it themselves, setting twelve children afoot on the prairie grass, a covey of McMurtrys who soon scattered like quail in the direction of the even emptier Panhandle.

The sense that resides in me most clearly when I think back on the twelve McMurtrys (all dead now) is of the intensity and depth of their hunger for land: American land, surveyed legal acreage that would relieve them of nomadism (and of the disenfranchisement of peasant Europe) and let everybody know that they were not shiftless people. (They came, like many other Scotch-Irish settlers in that region, from Missouri, against which there seemed to linger some slight prejudice; Missouri was thought to be lawless, a breeding ground for outlaws.) To the generation my grandparents belonged to, cut loose by the Civil War, all notions of permanence and respectability were inextricably woven into the dream of land tenure, or acreage that would always be holdable by themselves and their children. And yet the McMurtry boys who left the old folks and went to the Panhandle to seek—and get—land of their own were soon overtaken by irony and paradox. They got land, lots of it, yet what they had been before they *had* land—cowboys—beckoned them all their lives. It was the cowboy, a seminomadic figure who often owned nothing but a saddle, that gave rise to all the stories, all the songs, and many of the movies, when movies came. These aging ranchers, some of whose wild children were already well along in the process of losing the land they had worked so hard to acquire, had, at the end, as consolation for much loss and wastage, the knowledge that they had all, at least, been cowboys in their youth, men who had known the land when it was empty, a place of unpeopled horizons.

One of the things I have been doing, in twenty novels,

is filling that same emptiness, peopling it, trying to imagine what the word "frontier" meant to my grandparents (as opposed, say, to what it meant to Frederick Jackson Turner, already a coat-and-tie professor at the University of Wisconsin while my grandparents were building their first cabin and begetting yet more McMurtry quail on that hill in Archer County).

Ironically—not to forget Walter Benjamin—in the very year of his birth (1892), a colony of German immigrants became neighbors of my grandparents in Archer County. A seventy-five-thousand-acre patch of prairie had somehow been secured by Bismarck's liberal foe Ludwig Windthorst; by 1895 some seventy-five German families had settled in an area only about seven miles from where my grandparents built their first cabin. The Germans worked hard, prospered, and are still there. For years I thought "Windthorst" meant something like "wind thrust" (it *is* a notably windy county), until I happened on a biography of Ludwig Windthorst, read it, and was enlightened. When young I merely accepted the fact that my father or my grandfather rode over horseback a couple of times a week, to get our mail at Mr. Weinzapfel's store.

Walter Benjamin, a man famously erudite (though not scholarly), was attempting to write about the storyteller in a broad context, as a figure in world—as opposed to European—history; and yet his description of the way good stories are told and passed on presupposes a certain human and cultural density. There must be people gathered in a place—ideally, perhaps, in an artisan's shop—to listen to the storyteller and to repeat the story in their turn.

What could he have made of my grandparents' situation, as it was when they had just arrived at the edge of nowhere? And (funnier question) what would my grandfather have made of the marathon that had been scheduled to be run down the road that passed our house, one hundred years (or almost) after he and my grandmother arrived? Though several of his children signally failed to learn to do anything but work, William Jefferson was no workaholic; he preferred shade to sunlight and, once in the shade, liked to ruminate, speculate, question, converse. The spectacle of a bunch of fools in shorts attempting to flounder along for twenty-six miles in the heat would no doubt have provoked some pungent ruminations.

Archer County was not completely unpopulated when my grandparents arrived, but if Walter Benjamin had happened to be in the wagon with them the day they stopped and unloaded by the fine seeping spring, I expect he would have found the locale to be a context of no context, not immediately propitious for storytelling. My grandfather loved to talk but, due to the absence of near neighbors, had mainly his wife and children to talk to. Louisa Francis, at least from my few observations, had little interest in his spoutings, and the journeymen, tinkers, mendicants, artisans that Benjamin thought made up a good audience for storytelling were at first a long trot down the road.

But they were there, William Jefferson and Louisa Francis, settled on a piece of land that didn't easily yield a living. The Comanches were no longer a threat, though only a few years earlier they had attacked and killed a little party of teamsters scarcely fifteen miles from where the first cabin stood. What my grandparents had to contend with was the sky and the sun, forces sufficient to drive many a pioneer family back to gentler climes.

When I came along, about a half century later, there were still only a few people to be seen, but life had nonetheless accumulated, in all its puzzling but pregnant detail. The covey of McMurtrys, all glamorous birds to me, had—except for my father—long since flown away. And yet, by then, there was a cook, a cowboy or two, my grandparents, occasional visitors (a fencing crew, a vet, a cattle buyer, a surveyor, an oil speculator), who, taken in the aggregate, comprised the beginnings of a sort of culture. In the evening, once the chores were done, people sat on the front porch (if it was summer) or around the fireplace (in the winter) and told stories.

None of these stories were ever told to or directed at me; none of the Slovenly Peter, this-is-a-warning-little-boy stories ever came my way. But I was allowed to listen to whatever stories the adults were telling one another. At that time radio had not come, and when it did come it was at first too staticky to be worth listening to. Except for the occasional square dance, no one had any entertainment *except* the exchanging of experience that occurs in storytelling. So it was, no doubt, in rural places throughout the centuries; then, there was no media—now, it seems, there's no life.

My question to Walter Benjamin would be, what kind of stories arise in a place where nothing has ever happened except, of course, the vagaries and vicissitudes of individual life? It was these vagaries and vicissitudes, individual in texture yet common to humanity, that usually got discussed on the porch after supper, a dribble of family history usually involving accidents, injuries, bad choices, good choices, mistakes made with horses, misjudgments of neighbors, and the like. None of this was as interesting to me as the mystery of the old skunk woman, the silent, heavy figure I had come to dread seeing on the road almost as much as I dreaded seeing another hitchhiker whom my father invariably picked up, in this case an unfortunate man—I think he too lived in a hovel, somewhere in the brush—afflicted with St. Vitus's dance. He gibbered loudly all the way to town but I could not understand a word of his gibbering.

The loud, broken-toothed man with St. Vitus's dance scared me, but it was the old skunk woman who haunted my dreams. There was a judgment in her silence that I could not fathom; but it was a terrible judgment, I felt, and I wondered often if I was included in it. Everybody— by which I mean our six or eight more or less near neighbors, "near" meaning within twenty miles—knew that she had been acquired for a bunch of polecat pelts. What, I wondered, had made her silent? From my young perspective she was not so much Mother Courage as Mother Hell.

5

☽ THEN THERE was the Dutchman (as the Germans were then invariably referred to) who lived up the road from us, one farm away. He was a well-liked man who didn't have much acreage or many dairy cows; he was respected by the cowboys because he worked so hard. One morning he went out to his barn as usual, milked his cows—this was well before the days of automated milking machines—and then picked up a shotgun and killed himself.

I remember the shock of that event because, up to then, it had never occurred to me that it was permissible, or even possible, to kill oneself. Up to that point—I was probably five at the time—I assumed that, once alive, you were required to stay alive until a horse fell on you or lightning struck you or something. It seemed to me that if you could avoid those two pitfalls, horses and lightning—I knew, already, two people who had been killed by lightning, a real peril to cowboys—you would live until you were old, like my grandparents. By that time my mother's parents had also come to live with us.

To the cowboys, though, the haunting element in the Dutchman's suicide was that he milked his cows first, every cow, and even strained the milk. This fact came up, time and again, during lulls in the work, as the cowboys, many of them fond, like my grandfather, of filling their idle moments with aimless whittling, casually whittled away stick after stick. (These whittling cowboys, their hands occupied but their minds in neutral, were, in Benjamin's terms, perfect receptacles for stories, though often, no storyteller being available, they were wasted receptacles.)

The fact of the suicide itself didn't puzzle or even particularly surprise the cowboys. Considering the well-known difficulties of dairy farming, killing oneself seemed to some of the cowboys a more or less practical act.

"That dairy farming, it's gloomy work," I remember one cowboy saying. "All them cows switching their old shitty tails in your face."

At the time I was too young to have milked a cow, but I didn't stay too young. A little later in life I came to agree that getting slapped in the face with a milk cow's shitty tail was a considerable aggravation, though not aggravation

27

enough to tempt me to put a shotgun to my head. I came to think that there had to have been more to it than the admitted frustrations of milking. The cowboys, though, had little interest in probing such mysteries. They could easily accept that life, particularly the dairy farming life, could get a man down and finally break him; but once broken, why bother milking the cows? Here opinion divided.

"If I was intending to blow my head off with a twelve-gauge, I'd be damned if I'd do the dern milking first," one said.

"No, now that was proper," another argued. "Them old Holsteins' bags will spoil if they ain't milked regular. It would just have made it that much harder on his wife. She'd have a dead husband and a bunch of ruined milk cows too."

The debate about the Dutchman's suicide dragged on for a year or two, surfacing whenever the cowboys had nothing more immediate to discuss; to my knowledge no consensus was ever reached about the dairy farmer who milked his cows before killing himself. After a while, to the cowboys he became just one of the dead—whether his last milking was an admirable adherence to duty or a piece of sheer folly was never decided.

But I never forgot the suicide of the nice Dutchman up the road. What was his despair, and why did it culminate just after milking on that particular morning? And his wife, about whom I know nothing? The cowboys never talked about her. To them the milk cows, not the wife, were the interesting part of the story.

6

◻ FIFTY YEARS later, less than a mile from where the farmer took his life, I ran into a milk cow while on my way home to my ranch house. I was driving a rented Lincoln, and the collision had interesting results—but I'll table that story for now, in the interest of getting back to the Dairy Queen, Walter Benjamin, and the Archer County centennial celebration. Stay in one place long enough, or return to the same place often enough, and some interesting ironies are likely to accumulate.

7

◻ MOST PIONEERS, faced with the sort of task my grandparents faced when they unloaded their wagon in the newborn Archer County, might have agreed with Henry Ford that history is bunk. Even if it isn't bunk, on the line of a new frontier there was no history ready to hand and no time to consider history's lessons, if it has any. But pioneers typically feel a little inferior to their more settled neighbors. They're the arrivistes—they have less, and they have to work extremely hard just to survive, to hold their meager ground.

In west Texas, at least, it seems to be at about the hundred-year point that the citizens of a county gradually acquire the notion that they ought to begin to be a little historically minded. Around the century mark, as citizens begin to remind themselves that there had once been giants on the earth—or if not giants, at least some pretty doughty settlers—the historical impulse begins to manifest itself. A list of early settlers will be drawn up, a county history written. If any old-timers still survive they will be hastily laundered and trotted out for the annual rodeo parade. If there's an empty shed or otherwise unusable building near the square, someone will probably take a notion to start a museum. All the above happened in Archer County. The museum is housed in the old jail, and the county history was written by my lifelong neighbor Jack Loftin, who long ago took it upon himself to establish historical markers at spots about the county where notable events had occurred. Some of Jack's short historical essays were written on the bottoms of barrels, which he then cut out and affixed to a handy post; often, though, he found nothing to write on except whatever large rocks lay near to the point of interest. The rocks containing Jack's notations are apt to be obscured by weeds or Johnsongrass in the summer, making historical inquiry, in Archer County, subject to seasonal variations.

Fortunately for history, the push to found an Archer County museum got under way about a decade before the mania for garage sales swept the land. The local museum is thus able to boast a few ancient tractors, a gas pump, various fragments of oil field equipment, a few harrows, my grandfather's last saddle, and a few well-rusted tools, all of which would have been seized by the garage-salers had they materialized a few years earlier.

The afternoon when I first read "The Storyteller" happened also to be the opening night for the county's ambitious historical pageant, conducted well after sundown, when the 116-degree heat had dropped to maybe 108 or 109. I went, and with freshened curiosity. I didn't hold out too much hope for the pageant as a dramatic event, but I had suddenly developed a desire to know something about the county's history, or at least what was thought to have been the county's history by the people staging the pageant. I was, at the time, probably the only novelist in the county (or maybe merely the only *published* novelist; for all I know there could be a hundred novels in manuscript scattered about the county—one for every methamphetamine lab, perhaps). The county's historical materials were *my* materials.

I wanted to know *(a)* what had happened in the county that was worth remembering, and *(b)* if so, did anyone still living remember it?

The answers, trickling in over the next few weeks, were *(a)* nothing, and *(b)* no one—which didn't keep the pageant from being enjoyable. It was held in the rodeo arena, under the deep skies and bright stars of a summer night, and was directed by a man from Brooklyn—a man who in fact made his living directing county historical pageants all over America. Such a man, in such a profession, must, I reflected, be in possession of much knowledge he would probably be happy to be relieved of. I figured his lot must be hard. A couple of weeks later, when he was at last Brooklyn bound, I flew with him from Wichita Falls to Dallas; he agreed that, yes, his lot was hard.

Hearing him sigh, I could not but marvel at what an extraordinary thing the American entertainment business is. Here was a man from Brooklyn, New York—perhaps a man who had brushed elbows with Norman Mailer on the sidewalk—flying around the country staging pageants that were supposed to dramatize the history of poky, late-formed counties in Texas, Nebraska, perhaps Idaho even, his performers all recruited locally from a restless body of housewives, county officials, roughnecks, truck drivers, and the like. If there was a lower rung of thespianism than this (nice) man occupied, it was not easy to imagine what it might be.

On our short flight the director, after heaving several sighs over his hard lot, and also swigging from time to time from a little flask which I imagine contained something stronger than sarsaparilla, asked me if I had enjoyed the show, and I was truthfully able to say that I had enjoyed it a lot. Breathes there the man with soul so dead that he could fail to enjoy a pageant held in a rodeo arena on a Texas summer night, particularly if the pageant attempted to dramatize the history of his own county from the creation of the universe through the Vietnam War? Fortunately the long geologic eras during which Archer County, as well as most of Texas, was covered by an ocean were dealt with expeditiously by means of a brief light show, shortly after which Cabeza de Vaca was put ashore in Texas and county history got seriously under way. With bold ingenuity several momentous historical figures—Adam and Eve, Columbus, Coronado, and the like, whose actual presence in the county has yet to be confirmed by historians, nonetheless trekked across the rodeo arena, where soon the local cowboys would be attempting to ride Brahma bulls.

On the whole, though, once creation and the discovery of Texas had been accomplished, the county's history quickly sped by. The cowboys soon defeated the Indians—or at least they soon did on most evenings. There were a few occasions when the Indians (most of whom were cowboys in real life) got tired of endless defeat, managed to unseat a few cowboys, and pummeled them soundly, to the astonishment of the crowd, who had not expected to be offered a form of revisionism for their five bucks. (In fact there were only two known Indian fights within the confines of what became the county, one in 1836 and another in 1870; neither was of much significance.)

The long, tragic struggle between mostly poor, hungry Scotch-Irish immigrants and the militant and determined aboriginals who held the land and fought bravely to keep it was reduced, in our pageants, to a few scuffles, as it had to be. Close on the heels of Indian history came church history; the spectators were left in no doubt as to the critical part religion played in the settling of the land. In fact, when the various local congregations got through reenacting their histories, the two world wars and Korea and Vietnam as well had to be disposed of rather hastily; then the county's dominant occupations, farming, cattle ranching, and oil, were briefly lumped in, after which the history-sated spectators rolled out of the stands and flung themselves into street dancing and other celebratory activities. Most of the people who saw the pageant seemed to think that one hundred years was a good long time for a place to be in existence. Thoughts of the more resonant antiquity of other civilizations—Egypt, China, Greece—probably didn't enter too many heads. When the pageant ended and the director took himself back to Brooklyn, the general feeling was that the history of Archer County had been given its full due—though, of course, everyone hoped there would be a lot more of it to come.

8

◯ "WHAT DISTINGUISHES the novel from all other forms of prose literature is that it neither comes from oral tradition nor goes into it. The birthplace of the novel is the solitary individual, who is no longer able to express himself by giving examples of his more important concerns, is himself uncounselled, and cannot counsel others." Thus Walter Benjamin again, making sure that no one confuses a novelist with a storyteller. The question I want to investigate is how someone like myself, growing up in a place that had just been settled, and a place, moreover, in which nothing of cultural or historical consequence had ever happened, became a novelist instead of being content to worry over an old woman who had been traded for skunk hides, or a dairy farmer who had given way to despair. Does mere human memory, the soil that nourishes storytelling, still have any use at all? What, in this age when we are all so oversupplied with information, does a given human need to remember, other than, perhaps, the names of his or her spouse (if any) and children?

My grandfather, for example, had a keen memory for weather signs, clues he picked up that others missed. Today he wouldn't need this skill: all he would have to do is turn on the Weather Channel. And of course, mere human memory has now been left in the dust by computer memory. This very week a computer named Big Blue, a machine with the capacity to remember 200 million chess moves, beat the current world champion, Gary Kasparov.

Big Blue not only beat him, it humiliated him. Except for the occasional Harold Bloom–like prodigy, computers can now easily remember more than humans remember. But then, fewer and fewer humans really need to remember very much. My grandfather, trying to survive on the frontier, *needed* to remember where water holes were and what weather signs meant; my father, a generation later, still consulted every authority he could find, from almanacs to county agents, before undertaking any major agricultural operation, such as castrating or dehorning calves. Now he could get far superior information from his vet's computer. One can dial up porn, or prayer, or medical advice with a like facility.

Even so, judgment is more complicated when you're dealing with living things, even stupid and unresponsive living things, such as cattle. Paul Valéry was right about the modern tendency to avoid any work that cannot be abbreviated; computers are abbreviation made manifest. They take a lot of the work out of work, which may be fine in some professions or occupations, but for a novelist to try to take the work out of work is profoundly self-defeating: keeping the work in work is all-important. I'm writing this book with a pen, unlike my twenty-two previous books, because I don't want the sentences to slip by so quickly that I don't notice them. They need to be the work of hand, eye, and ear. Here is Valéry again, in a comment on the work of a silk embroiderer:

> Artistic observation can attain an almost mystical depth. The objects on which it falls lose their names. Light and shade form very particular systems, present very individual questions which de-

pend upon no knowledge and are derived from no practice, but get their existence exclusively from a certain accord of the soul, the eye, and the hand of someone who was born to perceive them and evoke them in her own inner self.

Computers can probably now duplicate most of the work of eye and hand, but there's still the problem of the soul, though to say as much would be gilding matters a little in the case of myself and my pen, or, more commonly, my old Hermes typewriter. I didn't choose the Hermes because it accords with my soul, but because it accords with my hand. I just like the way the keys hit the page. They don't fight your fingers but you do have to put a little force in your stroke, so that forming a sentence is not entirely divorced from touch. There are also apt to be small imperfections in the ribbon or the inking, just enough so that the process of writing demands a little attention and some manual application.

That may seem—and be—an overly romantic view of typing and typewriters; by the same token Nicholson Baker's paean to the library card catalogues (now gone) was considered romantic by most librarians. One thing that I can say for sure about typewriters is that carrying one through an airport now attracts the eye of security people immediately. Typewriters have become rare, rather than common, accoutrements of travel. Nowadays few security people even know what one is; the occasional passenger who can still correctly identify this ancient artifact looks at me in amazement. "Why not just carry a roll of papyrus?" a perfect stranger asked me one day. The era of the traveling journalist with his or her Royal or Remington is clearly over.

9

☾ WHEN, IN the record heat of the summer of 1980, I began my little informal investigation of local memory and what it held, I was, as a novelist, mired in the Slough of Despond. I hadn't liked a word of my most recent novel, *Somebody's Darling,* and I wasn't, so far, liking a word of my next, *Cadillac Jack.* A little time off, during which I planned to casually inquire of the locals what they could actually remember of the country's majestic century-long history, seemed a relaxing thing to do. It could hardly have yielded worse results than I was getting in the meanwhile, as I slogged along from novel to novel. And by choosing the Dairy Queen as my field of research—my Amazon, my Olduvai Gorge—I would not only eventually encounter virtually everyone who lived in the county; I could stay cool doing it. I like heat, but I don't like the view from inside an oven, and the temperature, which climbed above a hundred for forty-two consecutive days that summer, made my old un-air-conditioned ranch house seem pretty ovenlike.

But in fact, as it turned out, my examination of local memory was over almost before it had begun. "Death is the sanctity . . . of everything the storyteller can tell," Benjamin says. "He has borrowed his authority from death"— and so it certainly seemed in Archer County, because all anyone could remember with any precision was the local deaths. Three boys were killed in a car wreck in 1954. A cowboy drowned in the Little Wichita River in 1956. A roughneck was blown off an oil rig in 1958; and so on. Sudden death, particularly death on the highway—as much a part of that culture as football—lodged in people's memories, whereas about almost everything else they were vague. A few people remembered that Lyndon Johnson had once visited the town briefly on a campaign tour. He landed on the courthouse lawn in his helicopter, with his (then) fat little daughters; somewhere along the way he had purchased a couple of bushels of peaches to give away. My father remembered to his dying day how small, cheap, and wormy those peaches were—he distrusted LBJ ever since.

All the men in town remembered that in 1964 the local football team won the state championship in their division, a feat commemorated by putting a small cannon on the courthouse lawn; the women of the community had mostly forgotten this triumph, though they agreed that whenever it happened, it had been generally a good thing.

I was surprised to find that even World War II was not really vivid in the county's memory. There were some veterans, but not too many; those with ties to the agricultural movement were mainly allowed to stay home and raise beef or grain. Benjamin remarks that after World War I, men returned home silent, poorer rather than richer in communicable experience; Marc Bloch, however, disagreed. Bloch's own feeling, as a combatant, was that the soldiers of World War I would believe almost anything except what was printed; experience passed mouth-to-mouth was readily believed. Be that as it may, the several cowboys I knew who fought in World War II seemed to have refitted themselves to civilian life by forgetting—or more probably suppressing—what they had seen and taken part in.

One departure for that war was particularly significant for me. My cousin Robert Hilburn stopped by our ranch house on his way to boot camp and left me a box of books, nineteen in all. These were the very first of the several hundred thousand books I have owned, as a reader and an antiquarian bookseller. I doubt that any gift has had a greater or more beneficial effect on my life. Those nineteen books were in essence my library until I entered Rice in 1954. Four years later Bob Hilburn returned from the Pacific theater. I was in the hospital at the time, with a mild pneumonia. He walked into my hospital room and handed me a Japanese rifle—I have it still, but I know nothing at all of Bob Hilburn's war experiences, or anyone else's, other than what I have read in books. The local cowboys who had been to war had more to say about their horses of the moment than they did about a world war.

Yet to me as a boy, World War II was an intense and constant experience, one that came to me largely through radio. One of the first radio voices I remember was that of Franklin Delano Roosevelt. The radio serials, as well as the comic books of the time, were, of course, intensely propagandistic. I didn't really know what civilization was, but I was fully persuaded that it hung in the balance those four years. I spent many hours on the platform at the top of our windmill, doing my duty as a junior plane spotter, in my hand vivid cutouts of all the enemy's aircraft, none of which, to my disappointment, ever appeared in the skies over Archer County. The Axis powers just did not seem to want to bomb the bulging silos of Windthorst. My grandfather was dead by D day but the rest of us sat around the radio all that day, my father even interrupting his work, to listen to staticky reports of the great doings on the Normandy beaches. It was the only time in my memory when world events were momentous enough to cause my father to stop his work, a fact which in itself did much to convince me that civilization's supreme hour was at hand.

We now have on the courthouse lawn a small wall on which are engraved the names of the county's war dead from—surprisingly, since there was no county here then—the Civil War on. This little wall is evidence of the force of what Maya Lin wrought with the great Vietnam memorial in Washington, though those who erected this one may not even have seen hers.

Walter Benjamin was a farseeing man, and a man with some experience in radio; but I suspect that even he would be a little surprised by the extent to which what's given us by the media *is* our memory now. The media not only supplies us with memories of all significant events (political, sporting, catastrophic) but edits those memories for us too. Anyone who has ever taken part in a large public demonstration—a civil rights march, a war protest—and then gone home to see the same demonstration as reconstructed by television will know what I mean. What to the participant may seem merely an inchoate surging of masses of people will look, on television, ordered and effective, though if there was any violence it will always be shown first. The eye of television is drawn to violence as the normal eye is drawn to the light in a jewel.

10

☼ I HAD the privilege, in 1960, of studying with the fine Irish short story writer Frank O'Connor. Mr. O'Connor was both a masterful practitioner and a thoughtful critic of the short story; his little book *The Lonely Voice* is for many the best study the form has yet had. But Frank O'Connor's subject was the written short story, not the oral narrative that Walter Benjamin was writing about. I often wonder what the two of them would have had to say to each other, could they have talked, for they were both skilled and passionate excluders, quick to say what was a short story and what wasn't. Frank O'Connor believed that most modern short stories were really compressed novels. If a given story tried to do something he felt stories couldn't do, he immediately dealt it out of the deck.

One of his most powerful convictions, one I have cause to recall almost every day, was that you couldn't make art out of unredeemed pain. Of course in our time that belief has a particular reference to the literature of the Holocaust, and I don't know that Mr. O'Connor was entirely right. Maybe you can make art out of unredeemed pain, but only if you're a genius—Dostoyevsky, perhaps.

The sin that television journalism signally must answer for is that of bringing the unredeemed pain of the whole planet into our daily lives. A village is buried by a mud slide in Peru. We see the small, hopeless people probing in the mud which has just buried their homes and killed their children. A man pulls up a pot, or perhaps a

41

child: he weeps. Or in Bangladesh a flood sweeps away eight thousand people and leaves countless thousands destitute and in the rain, possessed of nothing except their need. Or in New York a child is beaten to death by her mother's boyfriend—even Saul Bellow had trouble making child battering work in a novel. The rain of tragic images on television is unending. They drip into our lives every day, bringing neither the relief of dramatically realized tragedy nor even the fright of the fairy tale—through constant repetition the weight of the world's gloom increases proportionately.

In Kentucky, I recall, a man shot his television set and then himself during a news broadcast—he was a country man, like the Dutchman up the road who killed himself after milking. Did the Dutchman turn off the radio before blasting himself? I don't know.

11

☐ "THE ART of storytelling is nearing its end because the epic side of truth, wisdom, is dying out," Benjamin says. Well, maybe—but I did know an old mountain woman in a Virginia village whose storytelling would have pleased the exacting Berliner. She was eighty-six and had lived in the same house her entire life, never traveling more than six miles from home. If ever there was a local who stayed put, it was she. This old woman had surveyed almost the whole of the twentieth century from her front porch. The young men of the village went off to war; some came back and some didn't. Then another war came and the young men went off again. Washington, D.C., thirty miles away, was as remote to her as Hong Kong. She had no curiosity about it—the affairs of the village were all she had and all she needed. She had lived through the century of the motorcar traveling almost entirely by foot. But the local lore she knew: every house, every man and woman, and what had befallen them. She told many stories and told them well, but I would not be quick to elevate her stories above those of Frank O'Connor. Consider Ezra Pound's astonishment when he first saw Walt Disney's *Perri*. Why, it's sheer, absolute genius, he said.

An interesting way to test the resilience of a story is to watch any child old enough to switch channels with a TV remote—a skill that soon makes them greedy. Children now accept interrupted narrative—that is, commercials—as readily as we accept rain. Most of them will channel surf through commercials, looking for a flash of active narrative. They quickly develop a sure instinct for how long commercials last and will return unerringly to the main story just as it resumes. They are as much at ease with television's advancing technologies as I was, at the same age, with stick horses, and they early exhibit a keen devotion to the *exact* details of a story. If, for example, you dare to interrupt a five-year-old's thirty-ninth viewing of *The Lion King* in order to find out a basketball score, they will, once they regain control of the remote, immediately rewind the film to the point of interruption, so as not to miss the smallest element of the story. Watching the avidity with which the very young absorb stories—stories in books, stories on *Sesame Street,* stories on the cartoon network—leaves one no grounds for pessimism about the survival of narrative itself. The human appetite for it is too strong.

Even more heartening than the way children leapfrog commercials is the huge success of *Wishbone,* the PBS series in which a small debonair dog finds his way into the great stories of literature: Homer, *Don Quixote,* Dickens, Stevenson. The concentration with which children watch *Wishbone* should go a ways toward reassuring those who feel that literature is losing out in the competition for the attention of the coming generation. In fact, today's young, expanding imaginations are packed with a far more diverse set of characters and stories than mine was at a comparable age. In the forties my only access to the classics would have been through the always pallid Classic Comics. Now the young imagination is apt to be crammed with characters, both old and new: Odysseus and Don Quixote mix with Kermit the Frog, Bert and Ernie, Han Solo and Luke Skywalker—even, soon enough, Bart Simpson and Beavis and Butthead. The story-seeking children of today are far from impoverished.

12

◌ REMEMBER, THOUGH, that Walter Benjamin, in "The Storyteller," was writing at sunset. In four years he would be dead, and much more than an old mode of storytelling would die with him. I was a boy of four, with not yet even a radio to listen to, when he killed himself. A year later came Pearl Harbor—we had just acquired a radio. I remember that President Roosevelt's voice was almost drowned out by static. Another year and I was a junior plane spotter. Soon I would be making my way through the nineteen books that Bob Hilburn had left me, wondering what it meant that there was a war.

Fifty years of reading later I'm still to some extent wondering, having gained at best only a little sense of context. My grandfather died not long after Walter Benjamin—very little that was European clung to my grandfather, whereas almost nothing that wasn't European touched Walter Benjamin, who saw night settle on a world whose traditions were very old. He saw one sunset, my grandfather another—in his case it was the sunset of the American frontier. William Jefferson was of the last generation to settle on a Western frontier. My older uncles, though born in the nineteenth century, were not frontiersmen. They all made their fortunes in settled regions and ended their days as suburbanites. Frederick Jackson Turner chose 1893 as the year the frontier ended, by which time my grandparents had been in Texas almost a quarter of a century. William Jefferson McMurtry was breaking horses in Denton County when Custer fell. While my grandparents were dealing with almost absolute emptiness, both social and cultural, Europe was approaching an absolute (and perhaps intolerable) density. Walter Benjamin said Proust was the Nile of language; if he was the White Nile, then Virginia Woolf, in her diaries and letters, may have been the Blue—and joining these great waters were the long tributaries of Joyce, Lawrence, Musil, and many others. Most of my reading life has been a trip up those Niles, into the riverine abundance of European literature, much of it a long requiem, of which a late and serenely beautiful example is W. G. Sebald's *The Emigrants*. My social awareness was formed in a place that had been virgin land only a few decades earlier. Emptiness, space, vast skies, long horizons, and few people were my first facts, and for long, the dominant facts. My first seven years were spent entirely on the ranch, in a house built on a low hill in southeast Archer County, with the Great Plains stretching north all the way to Canada.

It seemed to me, as I read Proust and Woolf and the rest, that cultural density had the same power in the work of the European writers that the empty Western landscape had for me. Benjamin can scarcely write a paragraph without planting a quotation in it. He loved to quote and, early in his career, compiled an eloquent collection of German letters, only to have the publisher go bankrupt just as the book came out—most of the edition languished in a Swiss basement until the 1960s. (At almost the same time Nathanael West published his masterpiece, *Miss Lonelyhearts,* only to have *his* publisher, Horace Liveright, go broke just as the good reviews began to come in.)

The European writers could no more escape culture than I could escape geography. To this day if I attempt a rural setting I invariably reproduce the contours of the hill where I first walked. I started peopling my books in the place where my grandparents started peopling a new country. Departure and arrival, both good themes for the novelist, were slower then. Had Walter Benjamin lived to see the full development of international air travel he would no doubt have had something to say about what this extreme—and unprecedented—mobility means for the human psyche. (Now the Concorde has upped the ante even higher: we can skip to another continent and come back between breakfast and dinner. Julian Barnes has remarked on the peculiarity of traveling west on the evening Concorde and watching the plane overtake the sunset. I have had that experience myself, and yet, as a small boy, I often spent a good part of the day on the fourteen-mile horseback round trip to Windthorst, just to get the mail.)

How remarkable such a possibility would have seemed to my grandfather: traveling to Europe in less time than it took him to go get the mail. Of course, his trips to Windthorst were apt to be stretched out if he could find anyone along the way who would stop and talk to him. His only complaint about his German neighbors was that they were a taciturn lot, unwilling to stop haying or plowing or fencing to have a long chat with him.

In my grandfather's time the life of my old neighbor in Virginia, a woman who lived eighty-six years in the same house, would not have been uncommon; in my grandson's time lives that are tricoastal or even tricontinental will be just as common.

13

MY FATHER, who died in 1976, was haunted all his life by the privations his mother endured as a frontier woman. He never forgot the sight of her carrying water from the spring to the cabin they still lived in when he was a boy. Eventually a well was dug and water more easily coaxed from the earth, but to the end of his days, my father found it difficult to forgive women the ease of modern arrangements—something as simple as tap water. The old woman, Louisa Francis, recognized my father's unease and used it, becoming a gifted martyr and exploiting his sense of guilt.

I began to sense the drift of this common story of mother dominance when I was very young. The year of my birth, 1936, was the trough of the Great Depression. My parents married with no money—they lived, as was common in those desperate years, with his parents, in a simple ranch house built from a design supplied by Montgomery Ward. Louisa Francis, who had forthrightly run her own daughters off as soon as she considered them able to fend for themselves, was not pleased to have a pretty young woman, my mother, under her roof. My mother, not unnaturally, wanted to make herself useful, but she was up against a woman who had raised twelve children on a naked frontier with a not always sober husband—she had no chance. One morning, annoyed by some domestic trifle, Louisa Francis slapped my mother, a slap that echoed through my parents' marriage until the marriage collapsed, forty-four years later. My parents, like the Tolstoys, were thus sadly undone at the very outset of a long marriage. In the Tolstoys' case it was the too-frank diaries that the young count insisted his sheltered bride read; in my parents' it was a slap in the kitchen, occasioned by some trifling argument over who would cook my father's breakfast.

And that was that. My father built us a little three-room house, some fifty yards south of his mother's house, and there we lived. But the damage was done. When, forty years later, I would journey to Texas to attempt to stop my parents' Tolstoyan battling, the discussion of what they were fighting about would slide, within minutes, back through forty years of ragged incompatibility to the slap in the kitchen, in 1935.

I was affected and wary, as any child would be, by the long undercurrent of disharmony in my parents' lives, but the slap in the kitchen was one of only two or three things I knew about their lives that had the quality of a novelistic moment—though I never used it in a novel. In a way the seriousness of that slap in the lives of my parents is suggested only by an absence of slaps in my fiction.

On their forty-fourth wedding anniversary I brought them to Washington, mainly in hopes of calming them down for a day or two. They got through the anniversary without speaking a word to each other and flew back home the next day, to resume quarreling, which they continued with only the briefest remissions until my father died. Someone with the gift of William Trevor or the late V. S. Pritchett might have made a short story of my parents' forty-fourth wedding anniversary, but not me. Fortunately, in their younger years and their middle years as well they did seem to have a good deal of normal fun, square-dancing, playing cards or dominoes with friends, visiting and being visited. But the core problem remained: my father could not forgive my mother for having an easier life than his mother had.

14

☐ WELL BEFORE I came of age, or even to articulate consciousness, that romantic nomad the American cowboy had been fenced and confined. Highways, fences, farms, and roads large and small made a patchwork of the once spacious prairies. Only in a few large ranches in Montana, Wyoming, Nevada, and New Mexico are cattle still moved from summer to winter pastures in the old, nomadic way. The seasonal movement of animals, such as still practiced with reindeer in Lapland, horses in Mongolia, camels in some places, sheep and goats in many places, is no longer necessary in America; as a means of tribal survival it has rarely been necessary. The long cattle drives that took place for about twenty years after the Civil War were large commercial ventures, initiated by cattle barons (or in many cases, would-be cattle barons); they were not tribal efforts and, once the longhorns passed, did not even involve native cattle—or cattle like the Mexican longhorns, which had come to seem native from having been herded for over three hundred years.

The myth of the American cowboy was born of a brief twenty years' activity just before railroads crisscrossed the continent north–south and east–west, making the slow movement of livestock impractical. The romantic phase of cowboying ended well before my father was born, and yet its legacy of habit, costume, assumption, and to a reduced extent, practice formed the whole of the world I was born into in 1936. Oil production was, and for some time had been, the dominant factor in the county economically, but oil drilling was not to acquire much social or stylistic weight for another forty years. Oil didn't arrive at full respectability until oilmen were secure enough financially that they began to buy ranches: before long oilmen, along with doctors, lawyers, and a few insurance men, seemed to own all the ranches.

I had no notion, as a boy—not the faintest—that I would end up a writer. It was not until my cousin went to war and left me those nineteen books that I even had a book to read; but I *did* know, early on, that I would have to deal with cowboying, either successfully or unsuccessfully, because there was nothing else in sight. I was given a horse at age three, and didn't take leave of cowboying until I was twenty-three. For twenty years I worked with my father and with the eight or nine ranchers with whom we swapped work. I realized early on that it would be unsuccess that awaited me because of my profound disinterest in cows. As soon as I got those nineteen books I began a subversive, deeply engrossing secret life as a reader. I very soon knew that reading would be the central and stable activity of my life, and that making a living would have to be made to fit in somehow, but if I could help it, it would not involve cows.

I mainly liked the cowboys I worked with when I was young, but I sensed early on that we were only nominally of the same species. I didn't pop books into my saddlebags or my chaps pocket to read at lunchtime or when there were breaks in the work. There weren't many such breaks anyway—my father was a firm believer in putting in a full day's work. Even though I never read while working cattle, I was soon thought to be a bookish boy anyway, and neither my father nor anyone else invested much hope in my future as a cowboy. They were possessed of enough savvy, those cowboys, to figure out immediately that I wasn't going to be doing what they did for a living—not for long.

The cowboys didn't care whether I stayed with their way of life or not, but for my father it was a trickier call. He knew early on that the ranching tradition to which he and his brothers had devoted their lives was doomed. He survived in it through hard work and great skill, but even so, had been in debt for fifty-five consecutive years and, at his death, still owned only four sections of land—not enough, in an arid region, to make any rancher much of a living. He knew that ranching had ceased to be a viable profession for smallholders or, really, for large holders either. (Although he knew that many cattlemen even in the days of the open range had gone broke, I'm not sure he understood that the range cattle business had never really been a secure profession, at least not on the central plains, mainly because the cattlemen had brought the wrong animal—English cattle—to an arid grassland to which they were not well suited. South Texas cattlemen, raising Mexican longhorns that *were* well adapted to their environment, did, on the whole, much better.)

Still, ranching was the only craft my father knew and his devotion to it was deep. It was not easy for him to live out a working life knowing that what he was working at would not survive him. It was, for him, tragic that the work he loved most—the outdoor work with men and horses—was not going to last beyond his time; the traditions it had bred would soon die with the work. It had only really lasted two generations, his father's and his own.

He had read a bit about the American West, but other than that had not much history. The history that mattered to him was the history his own family had lived, from the day William Jefferson and Louisa Francis unloaded their wagon on that hill. Of the larger and much longer history of men and ruminants, the droving, herding, pastoral nomadism that lay behind cowboying—centuries behind it—he knew little. Yet the movement of men and animals over the earth is an old and powerful thing; its hold on my father and all the cowboys I've known was deep. At a second remove, through the movies, it has held millions who weren't cowboys. The seeming freedom of nomadism, the movement of men and herds over the plains of the world, under spacious skies, retains a strong attraction even now, for people who will never know it at close hand as my father and his companions knew it.

There was no way and no reason for my father to escape the power of this tradition, since he was skilled enough even as a smallholder to survive within it. In an increasingly suburban world it was gratifying to him to feel that he could do his work with men and horses and answer to no man directly. But the fact of debt was always there: he escaped offices and time clocks, but not economics. An instructive text in this regard is Wilfred Thesiger's great *Arabian Sands,* the book about his travels with the Bedouin, by foot and camel, across the Empty Quarter of Arabia. Here were nomads who had to contend every day with the power of a great desert, a force far more threatening than a bank in Wichita Falls. At stake for them was life itself, not next year's loan. Yet they thought of themselves as the freest of the free—as long as they had camels they could go where they pleased, just as the cowboy once could on his horse. They considered themselves blessed and so did most of the cowboys I have known. Like the Bedouin they owned very little, but they always had the freedom of the skies.

My own fate, in relation to the cowboy, has been more complicated than my father's. Some years ago, in a piece in *Esquire,* as I was attempting to explain why I liked to drive back and forth across America on the interstates, I suddenly realized that I hadn't escaped cowboying at all. What was I doing, proceeding north on I-35, but driving the trucks and cars ahead of me up to their northern pastures? My driving was a form of nomadism, and the vehicles ahead of me were my great herds.

Suddenly I saw how much my Cadillac cowboying explained. Unfit for ranch work because of my indifference to cattle—if sent to fetch a particular animal I usually came back with the wrong one—I went instead into the antiquarian book trade, becoming, in effect, a book rancher, herding books into larger and larger ranches (I now have filled a whole town with them, my equivalent of the King Ranch). I couldn't find the right cow, but I *could* find the right books, extricating them from the once dense thickets of America's antiquarian bookshops.

But the metaphor of herding can be pushed even further, to writing itself: what is it but a way of herding words? First I try to herd a few desirable words into a sentence, and then I corral them into small pastures called paragraphs, before spreading them across the spacious ranges of a novel.

Even the fact that I've now spent most of a working life herding words in the morning and secondhand books in the afternoon still doesn't encompass the full range of my involvement with the American cowboy and his Eden, the unfenced, unsettled nineteenth-century West. I began to write fiction and resisted dipping (or slipping) back into the nineteenth century for almost thirty years. Even when I was writing *Lonesome Dove* I didn't feel that I was writing about the Old West, in capital letters—I was merely writing about my grandfather's time, and my uncles', none of whom seemed like men of another time to me.

Since then, though, I've written six novels, many screenplays, and two miniseries set in the nineteenth-century West. This may have been due, in part, to the human tendency to look farther back as one gets older; it may also be because I had exhausted the contemporary themes I felt most interested in.

My experience with *Lonesome Dove* and its various sequels and prequels convinced me that the core of the Western myth—that cowboys are brave and cowboys are free—is essentially unassailable. I thought of *Lonesome Dove* as demythicizing, but instead it became a kind of American Arthuriad, overflowing the bounds of genre in many curious ways. In two lesser novels, *Anything for Billy* and *Buffalo Girls,* about Billy the Kid and Calamity Jane, respectively, I tried to subvert the Western myth with irony and parody, with no better results. Readers don't want to know and can't be made to see how difficult and destructive life in the Old West really was. Lies about the West are more important to them than truths, which is why the popularity of the pulpers—Louis L'Amour particularly—has never dimmed.

In the end my father's career and my own were not as different as I had once thought. He cattle ranched in a time he didn't like much, and I word ranched, describing the time he longed to have lived in and the kind of cowboys he would have liked to know. He died about a decade before *Lonesome Dove* and never knew that one of his central desires—to be a trail driver—had found its way into one of my books.

I FIND it a little painful to be among cowboys now— of course, there are not very many of them to be among. Those who survive are anachronisms, and they know it. Most of them live in suburban hells, and yet are stuck with a style that lost its pith more than one hundred years ago. Many of the men who survive as cowboys now spend their lives being nostalgic for an experience—the trail drives—

that even their grandfathers missed. Rodeo, the only part of that experience that is accessible to the public, is a kind of caricature of cowboying.

The fact is, the American West was settled in one long lifetime. From Lewis and Clark to Wounded Knee is less than ninety years; the pioneer cattleman Charles Goodnight lived longer, and so did the plains historian Angie Debo. Well before the Custer battle, that shrewd entrepreneur William F. Cody (Buffalo Bill) was already putting on Wild West Shows for people who had never been, and would never be, west of New Jersey. What Buffalo Bill did to the Western experience was not unlike what television did to the Vietnam protests: he synopsized it. An Indian here, a stagecoach there, the Pony Express, a little trick riding, a few buffalo, Annie Oakley. It sold and it still sells—the stagecoaches still race at the Calgary Stampede.

What rodeos, movies, Western art, and pulp fiction all miss is the overwhelming loneliness of the westering experience. When my uncles (and even my father, for a year or two) were cowboying in the Panhandle they would eagerly ride horseback as much as thirty-five miles to a dance or a social, and then ride back and be ready to work at dawn. In Montana, Nebraska, Wyoming, the distances were even greater. Many Westerners were alone so much that loneliness was just in them, to a degree that finally made domestic and social relations difficult, if not secondary. The old joke that cowboys get along better with horses than they do with women is not a joke, it's a tragedy. The kinds of demands that the unfenced, unplowed, unwatered West made on human attention and human energy seemed to me to solitarize rather than socialize. Somehow the outlaw came to stand for this solitary Westerner—the man who has no ties because he kills. More common was the man who had no ties because he would rather work and keep working.

⌐⌐

FOR A time my first book of essays, *In a Narrow Grave,* was called *The Cowboy in the Suburbs* because that was its theme. What better symbol of suburbia than the Circle Ks and 7-Elevens that can now be found in even small and remote Western towns. In even fairly isolated communities people now take for granted the suburban privilege of buying a six-pack or renting a video at three o'-clock in the morning.

⌐⌐

THE PROBLEM of the American cowboy perfectly illustrates the classic problem of the field anthropologist: as soon as you find an unstudied tribe and introduce yourself to it, it ceases to be the tribe you found. The purest cowboys were those fourteen- and fifteen-year-old drovers who went up the trail with the first major herds in 1866 and the years just following, when the practice of trail driving flourished. A decade later Wild West Shows were going concerns and a voluminous pulp literature had developed: dime novels, the literature parodied in *Anything for Billy.* Teddy Blue reports that cowboys read pulp cowboy stories as avidly as any Eastern dude. Thus almost at the outset cowboys began to try to cultivate an image that the media told them was theirs—they began to play to the camera as soon as the camera was there, and the camera, for a long time, has been ubiquitous. In one year I was asked to write forewords or introductions to no less than nine books of photographs about cowboys or Western ranch life. One of these got introduced by Tom McGuane, another by Louis L'Amour, the industrious pulper who spent a good part of his life hoping that people would mistake him for a realist. The people who asked for the introductions were mostly shocked to discover that I didn't love cowboys and didn't want to wax poetical about them. (There can be few cowboys left in the West who have not been photographed for one or more of these books. The ranch women have also been photographed, as has much of the livestock.) The one book of photographs I *did* decide to write about was Richard Avedon's *In the American West,* a book I liked at once because it was so brutally antipastoral, so true to the gritty West of drifters and pig farmers, of truck stop girls and truckers; it was the book that put a period to the long tradition, begun by Alexander Gardner and William H. Jackson, John Hillers, Timothy O'Sullivan, and in this century, particularly by Ansel Adams, of seeing the West as one vast glorious pastoral landscape. Though those pictures may be wonderful they are in most cases empty of the often sad, more or less mute, inglorious humans who actually inhabit the great landscapes.

⌂

COWBOYS, EARLY and late, have been influenced by their own imitations, in pulp fiction, in movies, in rodeo. For a time young cowboys aspired to own Larry Mahan boots as avidly as young basketball players aspire to own Air Jordans. There is a difference, though: rodeo remains a marginal sport, hermetic even; it produces few stars potent enough to sell a line of boots or a variant on the ever popular Levi's. The designer Bill Blass recently remarked that no designer in history—not Chanel, not Dior, not Saint Laurent—had had an impact on world fashion even remotely comparable to that of the designer of the blue jean.

15

IT'S A pity Walter Benjamin never got around to writing an anatomy of memory, with attention paid to the way our memories function—or don't—at different stages of life. Mine is now at the stage where it's making, perhaps a little precociously, a kind of backward arc, giving me a focus on the early decades of my life that is much sharper than anything I can bring to bear on the events of the more recent years. In American memory the cowboy is generally idealized, even if the only cowboys the American has ever seen were on a movie screen. Cowboys are thought to be fearless, whereas my years as a cowboy were predominantly fearful. Nothing that happened to me personally ever fit the archetype. I grew up on a rocky hill with an abundance of rattlesnakes yet never had a close brush with a snake. Stampedes are a staple of Western autobiography, generally made to seem terrifying. And yet I participated merrily in such modest stampedes as came my way, racing happily along beside the cattle, glad for a break in the boredom of watching these same cattle plod dully along toward wherever we were taking them.

Throughout my cowboy childhood the contrast between what I *should* have been afraid of—snakes, bulls, stampedes—and what I was actually afraid of—poultry and shrubbery—was ignominious. The most frightening factor in my early childhood, hands down, was poultry, with trees and shrubs a close second.

At the age of four, while attempting to follow my father into a mesquite thicket, with the pathetic pony I had been assigned running as fast as he could, I smacked right into a yellow jackets' nest; the wasps—a good deal faster than my pony—stung me twelve times about the head and shoulders. Nowadays I would probably have been rushed to an emergency room, but the nearest hospital was then about forty miles from the pasture where the wasps struck. My father—though concerned that I had come off badly in this encounter with the yellow jackets—was not disposed to stop work and seek medical assistance. All that happened was that I was sent to the house for the afternoon, accompanied by Jesse Brewer, an old cowboy who had been hired to look after me. Jesse was my Jeeves, in a sense; he was supposed to keep me out of serious trouble, or at least to see that I kept a stiff upper lip if serious trouble came along. Unfortunately for that aspect of his mission, Jesse himself was incapable of keeping a stiff upper lip, being given to lachrymose fits himself at the contemplation of his own (in his view) misspent life. Besides that, he was only occasionally capable of controlling his horse, a large bay gelding who frequently took the bit in his teeth and raced away over hill and dale (or in this case, rocks and stumps) with Jesse sawing helplessly at the reins. As soon as the big bay carried Jesse away my base-minded little pony would either attempt to bite me, scrape me off against a tree, or fling himself down and attempt to roll over on me. Often, at such times, with my valet and gun bearer miles away, I would simply dismount and walk home, leaving my despised pony to his own devices.

After the encounter with the yellow jackets I did my best to avoid trees, but there was no avoiding the primary terror of my childhood: poultry. It was the Depression and we were many miles from a grocery store, which didn't matter, since no one then would have been disposed to squander money on store-bought food. We grew or raised virtually everything we ate, and kept what seemed to me profligate, overabundant flocks of poultry: normal chickens, game chickens, guinea hens, turkeys, and even a couple of peacocks. Many of the scratchy farms in the area kept a peacock or two. Probably to old ranch women like my grandmother the peacocks represented beauty, their glorious tail feathers the only relief available from dust and bleakness. (I doubt that my grandmother, in her whole life, spent as much as ten dollars on cosmetics or personal ornament of any kind.) Those raucous birds were much the prettiest things farm women had to look at then.

At any rate, toddling about amid the flocks of poultry, most of which were taller than I was and many of which were aggressive, I learned my first lesson, which was that human beings were peckable. The only hope was avoidance, but avoidance was not easy. I spent my days trying to thread a safe path through the hens, roosters, guineas, turkeys, game chickens, and peacocks. I was small and several of the birds were serious peckers; often my only option was wild flight across the vast reaches of the hill. I was one and the turkeys and hens were many; I was slow and they were swift; the result being that I often got pecked.

Though I hated the poultry, I did observe that these

domestic birds led short, uncertain lives. Sometimes the fox *did* get in the chicken house—sometimes an owl swooped down and took a pesky hen. The lives of pullets, particularly, were subject to abrupt termination. I was a cheerful witness to many summary executions, most of them performed by my grandmother with her hatchet; if lunchtime approached and she couldn't find her hatchet she would simply whirl the chicken around a few times and pop off its head. Often a pullet would be killed, plucked, cut up, and cooked before the head quite realized that something was seriously amiss.

When I attempt to think back to early childhood the scenes that spring to mind most vividly involve poultry, particularly one violent old tom turkey who would chase me whenever he saw me. I had no love for the pigs either, wallowing in their sea of mud by the barn, squealing, calculating, clearly malign. I was a young cowboy who hated his horse and feared almost every animal on the place. Those that didn't peck were apt to kick. The only animals I felt really kindly toward were our two brown mules, models of dignity and rectitude, more to be admired than even our one or two good horses.

Early on I realized the force of the place and loved the skies. I wasn't especially happy, being conscious too young of the gap between my abilities and what was expected of me, but I was securely *placed.* Here was the house, with its long porch on the east. There, a mile away, was Highway 281, a road that could take one north into the heart of the plains, or south to Mexico. I had never heard of Mexico then, but I could look across the mile of plain and see many cars and trucks, all going *somewhere*— places I too might someday go. Beside the house was the smokehouse, where dusky hams hung, and sides of beef. Near the smokehouse was the sunken, sunless stone cellar, a place my obsessive, cloud-watching mother forced us to huddle night after night, hiding from tornadoes that fortunately never came.

Beyond the cellar, some seventy-five yards west, was the barn, and south of that, the spring that had tempted my grandparents when they first arrived on the hill. The spring was bordered on the north by a thicket of tart wild plums, which yielded and still yield delicious jellies.

And beyond that lay the home place, two fields and a long pasture, supplemented, a little later, by some leased land a few miles down the road to the south by West Fork, a forbidding world timbered by a lot of stiff trees, post oak and elm mostly.

It was a modest world, nothing one could compare to the great ranches of the Panhandle, the Trans-Pecos, or south Texas, but it was so sharply and simply defined that it has, ever after, drawn a kind of border about my imagination, geographywise. I see that hill, those few buildings, that spring, the highway to the east, trees to the south, the limitless plain to the north, whenever I sit down to describe a place. I move from the hill to whatever place I'm then describing, whether it's south Texas or Las Vegas, but I always leave from that hill, the hill of youth. My father never left it, physically or otherwise. According to my son, who was with him, he spent the day before his death driving around the old hill, looking, remembering the family's life there, I expect: here was the spot where his brother Jim was crippled for life, here the place where two of his brothers dropped the barrel of molasses, which burst and allowed the winter's sweetening to soak into the ground.

Then, shortly after that drive around the hill that held his life, my father went home and died in the kitchen. But my son was with him that last day, and the potency of the place and its history passed from grandfather to grandson, as it should.

16

☐ IT IS well to remember that the first cowboys were Victorians. The values of the old queen traveled West, along with many of her subjects; several of the largest ranches in the West were established with English money. The values that came with the money, despite some snobbery, were very much the values that Baden-Powell wanted his Boy Scouts to emphasize and practice: honesty, courage, fidelity, and the like.

In my view the Victorian value which played the largest part in the settling of the American West was industry. I observed my father at work on a daily basis for many years and cannot imagine how a man could have worked harder, physically—and he did it virtually from the time he could walk until the morning when he died, in 1976. Of no one could it be more fairly said that dying was a kind of rest—perhaps, for him, the only kind he could accept.

The English Victorians, of course, left copious records of their industry. The American pioneers I knew when I was growing up worked far too hard to leave many written records: their records were their fields, their houses, the children, their herds. My grandfather, in the strictest sense of the word, started from scratch, in a place without a house, on land that had never been plowed. The effort to rear something there, something that wouldn't blow away—crops, buildings, children—used him up. My father and his brothers and sisters extended this same effort; theirs was the second phase, and they ended up living in small towns, in better houses; *their* children all went to school, a few even to college. Only when I went east in 1969, into the land of old money and powerfully Anglophilic traditions, did I begin to realize what starting from scratch really means. Of course there was Europe somewhere behind my grandparents, but it was a long way back and had been mainly rubbed out by several generations of frontier experience, as their people filtered through the Kentucky wilderness, into Missouri and finally Texas.

As I grew and read and learned a little about Europe, I began to try to understand what of Europe resided in my grandparents. My grandfather looked Scotch, but my grandmother didn't. Mixed in her was some Sioux blood, and also, perhaps, a good deal longer stay in Appalachia. When I try to think of what had been transplanted from the Old Country to that hill on the prairie, I cannot locate a single artifact or cultural accent that now seems European—unless it was my grandfather's pipe. I was keen early on for books but cannot remember a single book being in the house, not even a family Bible—if there had been a family Bible it probably burned up in a fire that consumed my grandparents' first frame house, which stood a bit west of the present ranch house. Anything else that might have come through some European ancestor was probably lost along the way of migration.

Almost as soon as I discovered Europe (in two books,

The Swiss Family Robinson and *Don Quixote*), I began to read my way toward it, an effort I have now been at for more than fifty years. Principally I was curious about the difference between new and old, and also the difference between dense and empty, open and closed, new country and old cities, no society and old society. I had a long road to travel intellectually but it was a very straight road, and—once I got to a place where there were books—a road that was very clearly marked. Traveling it was, for the most part, uncomplicated. The tradition I sought to leave—the cowboy tradition—was not yet even two generations old. Slipping away from it was as easy as slipping through a loosely strung barbed-wire fence.

So I slipped away, to Houston and the (then) Rice Institute, the Princeton of the South, and was soon securely placed in the world of books and learning. Houston, thanks to the timely invention of air-conditioning, had just begun to boom. In my time there it changed from a large, muggy Southern town into a dynamic city, more like L.A. than Atlanta; it was to experience some thirty years of wild and continuous growth, until, in the eighties, the boom finally broke.

Houston was my first city, my Alexandria, my Paris, my Oxford. At last I was in a place where I could begin to read, and I did, in Rice's spacious open-stack library. I didn't know that I was going to be a writer, nor did I suspect that the contrast between old and new, province and capital, wild and settled would occupy me for most of a writing life that has now passed the forty-year mark. I will, in time, go into more detail about the wiggle of my reading, through lives and centuries; I will only record now that every time I stepped into the Rice library I felt a mingled sense of security and stimulation—a rightness of some sort. I felt that I had found my intellectual home and began to relax in ways that had not been possible on the ranch, even after I got old enough not to have to worry about the poultry.

17

☐ ONE FINAL note about my early life in Archer County, as it related to what turned out to be a lifelong preoccupation with Europe. I have said that neither of my grandparents seemed to have anything European in them, but there were Europeans nearby, that is, the German people of Windthorst, people who had only recently left the old land and come to the new. Half a century had not taken Europe out of these people; they still had not, by the 1940s, become very American. Their posture—what we would now call their body language—was different from that of the cowboys and oil field roustabouts I knew. Even now, more than one hundred years after their arrival on the prairie, this is still true. I can spot a person from Windthorst by their more measured, more deliberate way of walking, and also by the extreme concentration they bring to their work habits. They might lack Bismarck's polish, but they still have Bismarck's energy. Many of them have become very successful farmers, thanks to their energy and their ability to concentrate it. For a whole century single families have applied themselves to a single piece of land, and this concentration has produced rich results. I don't think my grandfather or my father made any close friends among the transplanted Europeans, but they certainly respected the Germans' capacity for work. The suicidal dairy farmer who had had enough of toiling was a rare exception.

So at least some of the habits, tones, and flavors of Europe were just up the road—but when young I would never have evaluated that fact properly. My early understanding of place and my identification with it were structured in terms of occupation, not mentality or sensibility. I supposed the earth had been created mostly to be cattle range—our work—though I accepted that certain portions of it had been allotted to lesser occupations, such as farming or oil production. I felt that the reason the Germans seemed different from us was because they farmed, not because they were from Europe. But as I made my way through the public education system and into college, being taught fragments of history by teachers most of whom had never been more than three counties away, I nevertheless found Europe much more interesting than America. Maybe it was just that the names were more resonant. I soon got enough of Washington and Lincoln, not to mention Stephen F. Austin and Sam Houston. I wanted to know about Napoleon and Charlemagne, but so far as formal schooling was concerned, my curiosity had to wait.

Fortunately for me those were the days of the door-to-door salesman. Once we moved into Archer City—a move meant to spare me the rigors of an eighty-mile-a-day school bus ride—door-to-door salesmen began to arrive with their glamorous offerings, which might be a vacuum cleaner one day and an encyclopedia the next. In this manner—it was both the end of the Depression and the beginning of us as middle-class people—our household acquired two sets of books: *My Book House,* in ten volumes, a compendium of stories and legends from around the world (Charlemagne was there, along with Roland, King Arthur, Paul Bunyan, and Pecos Bill), and in twelve volumes, the *World Book Encyclopedia.* I was ecstatic: I wanted to know about history and here it was, at my fingertips. I had only to skip through the hundreds of articles until I puzzled it out.

It was not a bad way to begin learning; it may even have been an ideal way. When I skipped around in the *World Book* or in *My Book House* I was probably doing something not much different from what children do now when they channel surf. I think my parents must have been a little startled by the avidity with which I dove into the *World Book.* An investment designed mainly to help me with my schoolwork soon came to occupy me for hours at a time, even in the summer, when there was no homework. In attempting to do the respectable thing—become a household with an encyclopedia—my parents had unwittingly unleashed a demon; they may have sensed that all those words, on all those subjects, most of which could have no utility for a young cowboy in Texas, were what was going to take me away from the small safe town and the ranch on the hill. I remember my delight in the books themselves but also the slight beginnings of tension over what I ought to be doing with my time; the needs of a just-awakened intellect soon came into conflict with frontier utilitarianism, though not sharply. Once in a while it might be suggested that instead of reading I ought to be outside training the show calf I was supposed to be raising. But I think my parents realized immediately that such tactics had no chance. I was a reader, not a cowboy. I had none of the interest in cowboy accoutrements that most

young cowboys had. I was happy with any boots, any saddle, any spurs, or for that matter, any horse not actively
hostile to me. *My* fascination was with books, the way
they looked, hefted, were printed, smelled, and of course,
what was inside them. From the first I sought well-made
books. I had found my thing—reading—and never abandoned it (though it once abandoned me, of which more
later), and was substantially indifferent as to whether this
made me a sissy in the eyes of my peers (if it did it was only
to a slight degree). When I wanted to read, I read, however fine the weather or woefully untrained my show calf
might be, though I did have to yield to the necessities of
ranch work.

By the time I approached college age, paperbacks
had begun to filter into the local drugstore. I would occasionally slip a Signet paperback into the glove compart-
ment of the pickup but I rarely opened one of these unless
I was working alone and needed a break. If I had wanted to
read Max Brand or Luke Short or even J. Frank Dobie the
cowboys would have accepted it, but my taste at the time
ran to the most esoteric writing then available in paperback—the *Upanishads,* say, or the *Bhagavad Gita,* or the
Analects of Confucius, all texts I have never managed to
read. But if I had been caught trying to read them by the
cowboys, they would have considered that it meant I
ought to take off my spurs and check myself in at the nervous hospital.

I've not set out here to write an autobiography but
rather to describe the distance that separated me from the
European writers and historians I have spent so much of
my life reading. The gap, initially, seemed as wide as the
Staked Plain but, in the event, didn't seem hard to close.

18

☐ SPACE, A huge sky, and a sense of distance were things I simply took for granted, when I was growing up. It seemed natural that people should be widely spaced out—three or four miles to the nearest neighbor seemed a reasonable distance. I was unprepared for the crowdedness of cities, but I wasn't, at first, frustrated by it, perhaps because of the spaciousness of the Rice campus, then very open and sparsely built up. I was too excited to be in a place where there were books to notice that there were now, also, a million or so people in my neighborhood.

It wasn't until I moved to Virginia, to a pleasant valley near the Blue Ridge, that I first experienced sky deprivation, or forest claustrophobia. In Virginia I felt gloomy without knowing why—it was only after many drives home to Texas that the reason finally became clear. I began to notice that once I crossed the Mississippi at Memphis and began to proceed across the delta, the Arkansas flats, my spirits would suddenly lift. The sky had quickly opened up, become a Western sky, with Western horizons beneath it. Coming into that openness, time after time, brought relief and indeed a kind of exhilaration. This lifting (and a corresponding lowering as I drove back east) occurred many times; I began to understand that it bespoke a kind of sky longing which many Westerners have. The writer Richard Manning, in his excellent book *Grasslands*, mentions that he too experiences a lifting of spirit whenever he comes onto the Great Plains—he speculates that this

71

lifting of spirits may be an echo of the relief the unforested ape felt as he first stepped out onto the African plain and was suddenly able to see his enemies before they saw him.

Most writers who write about the West mention the skies often. In the forties the New Mexico writer Ross Calvin wrote a fine book called *Sky Determines,* a book largely about the accommodations living creatures—man included—have to make with aridity. It is partly an appreciation of the austere beauty of plains landscape, and partly a sociology of what it is the sky determines.

In the West lifting up one's eyes to the heavens can be a wise thing, for much of the land is ugly. The beauty of the sky is redemptive; its beauty prompts us to forgive the land its cruelty, its brutal power. Most farm and ranch people on the Great Plains are so accustomed to being victims of the skies that they can rarely find the time, or muster the detachment, just to sit on the porch and enjoy the skies for their beauty. "Lord, it's pretty here, on a summer night," one might say, watching a long, lingering, many-toned afterglow, but the subtle grays that come with winter are seldom noted. They were noted, though, by the early landscapists, George Catlin and Karl Bodmer particularly, both of whom responded to the power and the melancholy of the plains along the upper Missouri. As soon as painters were able to travel as far as the Rockies, dramatic if not overdramatic mountainscapes became the staple of Western art. The purest reaches of the plains were perhaps too close to nothingness to draw the painter's eye—the plains were and are minimalists' landscape; it is perhaps no wonder that artists such as Donald Judd and Agnes Martin were eventually so drawn to them.

I will never forget, myself, starting across the sere Oklahoma Panhandle at dusk one cold February evening and becoming so depressed by the melancholy of its emptiness that I almost had to turn back. It was perhaps because of that drive across the Oklahoma Panhandle at dusk in the winter that I began to read narratives of travel in Siberia, of which I now own about two hundred, among them George Kennan's little classic, *Tent Life in Siberia.* When a sky as vast as that over the Oklahoma Panhandle wears its foreboding aspect, lightness of spirit is not easily cultivated.

19

○ IT DOESN'T take much reading in pioneer autobiography to accept that my own aesthetician's love of Western sunlight is a very privileged affection. I've mainly always had these skies on my terms. My grandparents and their contemporaries had to take them as they came, and the way they came was not always benevolent. For them the sky was often an implacable destroyer: of their hopes, their crops, their economy, and their morale. The women who came west, like the men, had come mostly from English or quasi-English landscapes such as Virginia. They were used to responsive landscapes—gentle, forested lands, places where there was, if nothing else, at least an abundance of shade.

Then, suddenly, they were out on the plain or in the desert, where there was apt to be no shade at all. It might be too hot or too cold, it might be wet or it might be dry, but first and foremost, it was *bald.* Those who had always been shaded were suddenly exposed, and many of them stayed exposed until shade trees could be planted and given some years to grow.

The West has its grandeur, but there is nothing easy, nothing domestic about it. Shelter and domestic protection had to be secured with hard labor. Men and women went crazy in such country—it was harder, much harder, than they had supposed it would be. Many became deranged and had to be shipped back to places where there were asylums.

Of course, in dense, comfortable, faraway Europe, people were going crazy too, and doing it in such numbers that Dr. Freud had to invent a whole therapy for them: consider the Wittgenstein family, the Stephen family, the family of Ivy Compton-Burnett, to name only three. The great Lord Salisbury himself was prone to what he called "nerve storms," and Winston Churchill was hounded by the recurrent depression that he called his black dog.

Although there is an abundant diary literature piled up in state historical societies containing numerous accounts of hardships, child death, and general mortality in the West, not much has yet surfaced about prairie derangement. No one talked about it. All that was known was that a sister, a mother, a son would lose their reason and have to be sent back to whatever family had remained behind. There is nothing in the Western archives to equal the flood of madness memoirs out of Europe—memoirs which made it plain that the nerves of a whole, highly refined society were in a very deteriorated state; no wonder they were then shattered, collectively, by the cataclysm of the Great War. There is abundant evidence in a number of languages from Russia and Scandinavia down to the Balkans and along the Mediterranean that a very advanced society was having trouble keeping a grip on itself—and then, in 1914, it lost it.

Yet these years, from 1885 to 1914, seemed then to be the summertime of European serenity. Barbara Tuchman described this period vividly in *The Proud Tower.* The Souls were souling. The hyperactive Lord Curzon and the philosophically languid Arthur Balfour were in their ascendancy. (I have a copy of Balfour's speeches gracefully inscribed to Alice Roosevelt Longworth in 1912. Mr. Balfour's great parliamentary defeat in 1906 had not affected his handwriting. Henry Adams, by this time, could only produce a stroke-ridden scrawl.)

Elegance, wealth, power, confidence, polish hit a peak never approached since, and yet there was madness and depression within virtually every household. There was syphilitic Lord Randolph Churchill, and mad Nijinsky, and in Trieste, Svevo, trying to stop smoking. In Russia the Nabokovs were about to lose their Rolls-Royce, and everything else. The lonely Empress Elizabeth of Austria was soon to be stabbed by an anarchist, leaving old Franz Joseph to console himself with a chubby actress. Little Walter Benjamin, the born collector, was scouring the bookshops of Berlin, building his collection of early children's books, some of them quite close in tone to the once popular American comic strip *Katzenjammer Kids.*

Meanwhile, in Archer County, Louisa Francis was still carrying water from the seeping spring, but the trail herds no longer paused to water there, because there were no more trail herds. The railroads had come. There were still cowboys aplenty, though. Most of the McMurtry boys had left, to seek their fortunes. None of them went mad, though one or two of their wives did, and the last girl, Margaret, was always thought to be frail.

Context must ameliorate madness somewhat, but how much easier was it to be mad in London, rather than Archer County? Do the trappings of comfort—servants, doctors, even (for some) Dr. Freud himself—help the mad, or does all that merely increase their embarrassment?

I don't know about that, but I do know that writers touched with madness in London, Paris, Prague, Petersburg, Vienna, and elsewhere produced works of genius, whereas the mad ones of the Texas frontier produced only family sorrow. (The young novelist Dorothy Scarborough did produce one novel, *The Wind,* published anonymously in 1929, about a ranch wife who goes mad; D. W. Griffith filmed it with Lillian Gish. Dorothy Scarborough then went on to Columbia University and became a folklorist.) The crazies and near crazies of Europe produced literature; the crazies and near crazies of the Western plains mainly left a blank in the record of settlement. Not enough sand had seeped through the hourglass for them to have produced their madness memoirs. We are still less than two hundred years from Lewis and Clark, out here. How many centuries does it take to get from a pioneer family with all their possessions in a wagon to Proust and Virginia Woolf? It's certain that that sensibility, that spillage of language and flowering of nuance, doesn't soon emerge from rawness such as our Western pioneers experienced it. My father and his siblings attended school only when there were no flocks that needed tending or no crops to be sown or harvested—that is, for about three months a year.

Besides missing much of their schooling, they also missed the birth of the cinema. My father's first movie was a pie-throwing comedy seen in Wichita Falls in 1917, when he himself was seventeen. He became so hysterical with mirth that his embarrassed brothers carried him out of the theater, still laughing.

20

☐ A LITTLE more than half a century after my father saw that pie thrower, a movie company arrived in Archer City to film a novel of mine called *The Last Picture Show*. Though the movie, in the end, had little effect on the little town on the prairie, it had a cyclonic effect on the marriage of the director, Peter Bogdanovich, and his wife, the production designer Polly Platt. The cyclone, in this case, was not a cloud; it was a blonde, now known to the world simply as Cybill.

Seventeen years later most of the principals returned to the scene of their triumph (in itself usually a bad idea) to make a lugubrious sequel, *Texasville*, from the book of the same name.

To complicate matters more, an ancillary crew of documentarians led by George Hickenlooper arrived at the same time to make a movie about two movies, a witty little film that subtly shadowed the ill-hatched feature it aspired to document. It's called *Picture This*.

That made—in all—three movies and two novels set in the same small Texas town, adding onionlike layers of fiction to what was already the somewhat complex facts. Little wonder that Susan Sontag, visiting a little later, remarked that I seemed to be living in my own theme park.

She was right—the townspeople at times seemed under-standably confused, as parts of their own lives leaked into the film and parts of the film leaked right back into their lives. Some were extras, some had bit parts, some rented out buildings or houses; as time went on it became harder and harder to say where fiction started or fact left off. Some of the scenes had to be filmed in neighboring towns, so that to an extent the whole area leaked into the films, as it had into the books. So powerful was the experience that a few people began to suppose that they had been what they had not: I recently learned to my amazement that several impeccably matronly local women now think that they were the model for Charlene, the gum-chewing teenager who hangs her bra from the pickup's rearview mirror in *The Last Picture Show*.

Thus in ninety years the county had gone from unbro-ken prairie to Hollywood confusion and back again. The sets were struck, the Hollywooders left, the locals re-turned to the dreamtime. They had seen themselves, briefly, in the mirror of art, and had not been particularly interested.

In the end I suspect it may be that the Hollywooders were more affected by their time in the little town on the prairie than the town was by them. The Bogdanovich-Platt marriage ended and the Bogdanovich-Shepherd romance began. Without quite noticing it at the time, the people who told the tale got trapped in it—far more so than the people of Archer City.

In *Picture This* the trapped-teller motif is made sadly explicit. There sit Platt, Bogdanovich, Shepherd right in front of the burned-out marquee of the old picture show, talking about the marriage-affair-divorce of long ago as if it had changed the world, rather than just their lives. There were Tim Bottoms and Randy Quaid, looking like aliens who had just arrived on a dead planet, talking about their hopes and disappointments in regard to Cybill, and there sat Cybill herself, focus of thousands if not millions of fantasies, firmly rejecting regret vis-à-vis the Bogdanoviches' shattered marriage, even as her star maker, Peter B., only moments later, expressed vast regret. Instead of them defining Archer City, in the few weeks they were there it was as if the brutally bleak landscape had smashed them flat and doomed them all to keep looking into cameras and talking about themselves forever, describing themselves as they once were, or once might have been or hoped to be.

21

☐ ONCE IN Birney, Montana, while making inquiries about the Cheyenne resistance to strip mining, I had occasion to listen to the oldest woman in the Cheyenne tribe, old Mrs. Elk Shoulders, tell the story of the heroic long march of the Northern Cheyenne, from their exile in Oklahoma back to Montana—indeed, to within a few blocks of where we were sitting when Mrs. Elk Shoulders poured out her epic remembrance. At the time—not understanding Cheyenne—I thought she was angry with me for intruding on her privacy. It was only when I received a translation of the tape made that day that I understood I had been listening to an epic. My experience that morning in Montana is the only time in my life when I could feel I had participated in an epic narration done in the old way, with studied cadences and much repetition. (The epic event that it described—the long march—is told again in Mari Sandoz's *Cheyenne Autumn;* there is a film of the same name by John Ford.)

But to return to my question: how many centuries of settled urban experience does it take to produce a Proust or a Virginia Woolf? Might it be that the cultural fertilizers are so powerful now that such high sensibilities can be grown in a generation or two, rather than accreting sensibility a grain or two at a time through many centuries? Anyone of my generation, with a reasonably lengthy life experience, cannot fail to notice how quickly young children now advance in cultural fluency, drawing information, character, myth from every facet of this pluralistic, media-soaked culture. The young take what they want from the media as casually as one might pick an orange from a fruit stand. Bright children nowadays know more at a younger age than ever before, and television is in large part responsible. Whatever its defects, television brings the world to the young while they are young; and along with this, the ability to jump horizons and to experience, to an extent, the life of the whole globe has been advanced not a little by cheap airfare. I was nearly thirty before I made it from Texas to New York City, and nearly forty before I traveled much in Europe. My son, by contrast, had seen both Europe and South America before he was twelve, and my grandson, at six, is already a relaxed internationalist.

Of course, cultural fluency and ease of access to the whole planet brings with it no guarantee of either talent or depth. I grew up very limited but with a very straight road to travel, the road to education. I needed only to go where the books were, and I went. I was not deflected, dazzled, or confused by the smorgasbord of cultural options that the youth of today are faced with. When I left for college I had never seen a television program, heard a symphony orchestra, been in an art museum, visited a great city, or done anything much besides cowboy, read paperbacks, and listen to the radio. The range of seductions offered by the media now were unavailable to me. The materials of fantasy were consequently more limited, possibly beneficially so. I didn't have to wonder whether to try to be a rock star, a superathlete, or an anchorman.

The American West has so far produced depressingly little in the way of literature. Out of it may have come a hundred or so good books, a dozen or so very good books; but it has not, as yet, yielded up a great book. In literature it seems still to be waiting its turn. At the beginning of the century the Midwest seemed dominant, in terms of literary gifts and literary energies; then, largely because of Faulkner, the South had a turn, after which the great concentration of American literary energy returned to where it had mainly always been, the East.

Lately, looking through the various collections of photographs by the early photographers of the West—Alexander Gardner, John Hillers, Timothy O'Sullivan, William H. Jackson, and the others—it occurred to me that one reason the West hasn't quite got a literature was in part because the camera arrived just when it did. The first photographs were taken in the West only about forty years after Lewis and Clark made their remarkable trek. By the 1850s there were cameras everywhere, and the romantic landscapes of Catlin, Bodmer, Miller, Moran, and the rest gave way to photography that was almost equally romantic—the photographers, quite naturally, gravitated to the beauty spots, to the grandeur of Yosemite, Grand Canyon, Canyon de Chelly.

Writers weren't needed, in quite the same way, once the camera came. They didn't need to explain and describe the West to Easterners because the Easterners could, very soon, look at those pictures and see it for themselves. And what they saw was a West with the inconveniences—the dust, the heat, the distances—removed.

The first photographs of Plains Indians to reach the East must have been startling to the populace because many of the Indians were so handsome, so striking. Seeing them in their robes of state, as it were—the very personification of the noble savage—must have awakened at least a little ambivalence in the viewers, for the pictures themselves contradicted some of the most wildly propagandistic aspects of the rhetoric of conquest. Here indeed were the people Rousseau had been talking about, and yet the military men and the journalists were describing these handsome specimens as murdering, scalping devils, a people deserving only swift and, if possible, total extermination. And yet a few people must have wondered—and even asked—why we were slaughtering these beautiful people.

Only a generation earlier the McKenney-Hall portraits of Native American chiefs had managed, through their glorified style of portraiture, to make living Indians seem as if they were people from an ancient past; those portraits were vivid without being at all immediate. But the photographs, as they began to filter back east, were as immediate as today's newspaper. This is how Red Cloud looked, they say, and this is Dull Knife, or Sitting Bull, or Satanta.

Of course, the settlers who had to face these same Indians unassisted, on the Indians' home ground, often in desperate conflict, were confronting a force the photographs didn't show. The Comanche who was about to scalp you and carry off your children would be unlikely to remind a settler of the handsome figures in the state photographs.

But as the land was settled, the cameras multiplied—we can *see* the nineteenth-century West with a clarity not available before. Though we think first of the great photographs of beauty spots such as Yosemite, many images were fixed of life that was not grand and labor that was not appealing. Photographs of vast hills of buffalo hides and of pyramids of heads and horns should have made it plain that genocide was being practiced on a species: and yet, such is the human capacity for *not* putting two and two together that almost everyone was surprised when, one day, there were suddenly no more buffalo left to kill.

Despite photographic evidence, economic evidence, and human evidence, it was in the main the poeticized, pastoral West that registered in the public eye. Realistic, even naturalistic evidence was ignored when possible. The increasing poverty and marginality of the tribal people is fully documented, and yet, as has so often been the case in America, reality has proven to be no match for salesmanship. Edward Curtis, in essence a kind of Longfellow of the camera, did at least document some eighty tribes, even if what the photographs showed us was a kind of Indian in the mist; though it should be said that Curtis's blue pictures of natives wearing tribal masks produce a very different image than the dreamy pictures of Indians in silhouette against the sky. The public far preferred the mist. The blue pictures suggest that life in the West had its surrealistic aspects, and that there were cultures on the continent that were not very Hiawatha-like.

Of course, all along, the native peoples were producing their own art, for themselves. Had Benjamin been able to visit one of the southwestern pueblos he would have found, well into this century, storytelling that went on in the old way; even if he had not been able to understand the stories themselves he would have understood the pots and the weaving, for pots and rugs are silent in the way he liked stories to be: just themselves, free of explanation.

Native craftsmanship had to wait almost a century before it was appreciated by the conquering culture, at which point it moved rapidly from neglect to overcelebration, the hallmark of which is not merely grave robbing but wide-scale faking, particularly of the much-sought-after Mimbres pottery.

Anyone who spends much time with the photography of the American West will receive a vivid lesson in how quickly world succeeded world. Many commentators have been startled to realize that only one long lifetime separated Lewis and Clark from the closing of the frontier. The photographs show it happening. Here is the Kansas prairie, here is Jim Bridger, here Kit Carson. There are a few Pawnees, a Cheyenne or two, and perhaps Red Cloud. Then we see Dodge City, a few frame structures going up along a wide, muddy street; now here is the town once it had become a great cattle-shipping center. Here are the wildest cowboys, the most famous marshals, the prettiest whores. Then there's Custer, and the long line of wagons filing into the Black Hills. Custer finds gold and soon there's Deadwood, mud, squalor, wagons, Hickok,

Calamity Jane. Then there's the Little Bighorn, Buffalo Bill, Sitting Bull, the Wild West Show. Finally, there are the frozen ghost dancers, dead and twisted in the snow at Wounded Knee.

Anyone who wants to understand the West as it changed through those nine decades from Lewis and Clark to Wounded Knee must be grateful for the photographs, even—or particularly—for the family album photographs that give a glimpse of how life was for particular people in that not very distant time.

Recently, for example, I looked at a photograph of myself standing on an overturned washtub sixty years ago. Probably it was taken on my third birthday: state photographs of me always required me to stand on that washtub, the galvanized surface of which would have been heated by the sun until it was hot enough to fry an egg—or a small boy. I don't remember who came to that birthday party but I do remember the heat from that galvanized washtub burning through my sandals.

This particular state photograph was taken in the year of Munich, and I was standing on a washtub that was still in common and constant use. Once the party was over the washtub would be returned to its place by the back door; dirty clothes would be put in it to soak before being wrung through a wringer—the last time I can recall such a thing as a clothes wringer being mentioned was during Watergate, when John Mitchell suggested that Katherine Graham might get her tit caught in one if she didn't back off. To me the fact that I grew up in an age of washtubs to some extent explains my pretechnological bent. Just as the hill supplied, inescapably, the geography of my imagination, simple tools and implements lodged their nomenclature so deeply in my synapses that sixty years have not shaken them out. For example, the icebox. In my childhood the iceman came twice a week; he would carry in, with his great tongs, two fifty-pound blocks of ice, which he would put in our icebox. In a few years the iceman gave way to refrigeration, but I still, now, say "icebox" when I mean "refrigerator."

Soon after the picture on the washtub was made came electricity, which produced an indoor brilliance far greater than kerosene lamps were capable of. With the new inventions came specialists to fix them when they broke down. A by-product of the new technologies was a great character, the domestic bungler, the man who can't manage to fix even the simplest gadget: Dagwood in the comics, Fibber McGee on radio, and eventually Ralph Kramden of *The Honeymooners*.

22

☐ IT IS interesting that two of the very best books to come out of the West both center on the Custer battle: Thomas Berger's *Little Big Man* and Evan S. Connell Jr.'s *Son of the Morning Star*. The first is a novel, the second a history told as a kind of mosaic of memory. The only other similarly powerful work dealing with any of the great stories or characters to come out of our long war with the native peoples is the wonderful Geronimo section of Leslie Marmon Silko's *Almanac of the Dead;* the other great Native American leaders—Captain Jack, Chief Joseph, Red Cloud, Spotted Tail, Sitting Bull, Crazy Horse, Quanah

Parker—are there in the histories but not in the fiction, and the same can be said for the colorful generation of mountain men that included Kit Carson, Jim Bridger, and Jedediah Smith.

Any number of notable Indian leaders were mowed down during this conflict—think of old Black Kettle, the peaceful Cheyenne who survived Sand Creek only to be killed on the Washita—but for the purposes of myth what was needed was a young white hero, and it turned out to be the brave but on the whole rascally George Armstrong Custer. The Indians' great victory on the field they called the Greasy Grass was immediately the subject of rancorous debate of the sort that always occurs when the forces of white civilization meet defeat at the hands of socially inferior or aboriginal armies. The British had similar trouble dealing with their defeats at the hands of the Boers, the Zulus, and the dervishes.

When the forces of the Mahdi wiped out General Gordon at Khartoum the British public demanded vengeance and got it on the field of Omdurman. The American public, after the wipeout of Custer and the Seventh Cavalry, demanded vengeance too but never got it in any clear-cut way, unless the massacre at Wounded Knee twenty-four years later was in some part revenge for Custer. In terms of myth the Custer battle became our *Song of Roland;* myth overlooks the fact that Custer was a glory hound and a fool who cost more than two hundred men their lives that day in 1876, on the Greasy Grass.

The Little Bighorn is always popularly described as Custer's defeat, never as the Indians' victory—though a glorious victory for the Sioux and Cheyennes and other tribes that participated, it was also a bittersweet victory, for the Indians knew that they would never be so united again, and knew, too, that such annihilation was something the whites could not ignore or gloss over.

23

☖ MY BACKWOODS uncle, Jeff Dobbs, knew two of the last great Native American holdouts, Geronimo and Quanah Parker, during their days at Fort Sill, in southern Oklahoma. Uncle Jeff had watched as stock contractors drove the monthly allotment of cattle into the pens at Fort Sill—once the cattle were slaughtered, the dexterity of the Indian children in chopping the small intestines into short, candylike strips impressed him.

Fort Sill, near Lawton, Oklahoma, is only eighty miles from the hill where Louisa Francis and William Jefferson settled. My uncle Jeff Dobbs is to me like the man who once saw Shelley plain—the fact that he had known Geronimo and Quanah Parker meant that his eyes had seen another time: the wild time.

Many there were, as the nineteenth century neared its end, and as the frontier closed forever, who began to wish that they could have it again, bring the great wild place back. They wished as old men to see, once more, the virgin land they had plowed, the open range they had fenced, the paradise they had conquered and destroyed. The memoir literature is overwhelmingly nostalgic, filled with remembrance of what a wonderful country the West had been when they first saw it: the grass, the game, the skies, the mountains and valleys.

Few of the real old-timers, though, really wanted to put the red man back: the struggle had been too hard; the outcome, in thousands of cases, either painful or fatal. Though it is plain to us now, reflecting in tranquillity, that the Indians had no chance, that was a fact scarcely evident to the first white settlers who faced them, many of whom were obliterated before they could erect even a first crude cabin. The Western conquest was, from the first, shot through with the paradox: the bigger the Indian victory, the surer it made the eventual defeat. The first explorers, marveling at the glories of the West, began to destroy those glories as soon as they got across the Mississippi.

24

⏓ EASTWARD, ACROSS the Atlantic, the warlords were piling up weaponry and preparing for a conflict whose slaughter would make the little massacres of the plains and mountains seem as nothing. What are the eighty men killed in the Fetterman massacre, or the losses at the Alamo, the Little Bighorn, Wounded Knee compared to the tens of thousands killed on the first day of the battle of the Somme? In the American West the agony was sharp but short: twenty minutes for the Fetterman massacre, perhaps an hour for the Little Bighorn, only thirteen days for the siege of the Alamo. It was left to the military strategists of the older societies to devise conflicts that, in duration and detail, paralleled the long works of Proust, Dickens, Tolstoy. Think of Verdun, Gallipoli, the siege of Leningrad.

25

⌀ PIONEERS, EVEN those of middle-class origin, couldn't necessarily afford to lay the ladies off, when they started their new lives out west. But as Ian Watt has sagely informed us, without lightly employed middle-class ladies who were not allowed to do the housework anymore, there was no readership of sufficient size to support publishers, booksellers, and novelists. Lone families such as my grandparents', with all their possessions in one wagon, had little time to spare for reading—but a nostalgia for reading *did* exist, and as soon as little towns were formed there were ladies' groups, Amity Clubs, Browning Societies, and the like. But books were heavy and would have taken up space in the wagon that was needed for axes and saws, hammers and harness, spades, churns, skillets, cook pots, and progeny.

The first fictions of any value to come out of the West were usually about the struggle of sensitive, art-minded souls to survive and assert themselves amid the discouragements of necessarily practical frontier society. Willa Cather, for example. There was generally not enough society to nurture a novelist of manners: Red Cloud, Nebraska, where Cather grew up, was not Bath, or Jane Austen country. The men spent all day with the axe and the plow and the women went from pregnancy to pregnancy, just trying to keep up with the chores.

It's really been the edges of the West, the gateway cities, that have produced the most interesting writers—

St. Louis particularly, because it was *the* gateway city, the starting point for most of the great treks and explorations. It was also the place the riches of the West poured into; in our century a number of literary voyagers have either lived in it or set out from it: Eliot, William Burroughs, Harold Brodkey, Stanley Elkin, William H. Gass.

The other Western city to be an early nurturer of writers was San Francisco, on what is now called the Pacific Rim. Twain, Bret Harte, Jack London, Frank Stockton, Frank Norris either were west or went west, though Twain soon came skipping back east, to be followed, in due course, by Willa Cather, Dreiser, Sinclair Lewis, Fitzgerald, Hemingway, and many more.

The interior West, in time, did produce writers who had long, if for the most part odd, careers: Vardis Fisher, Frederick Manfred, Wright Morris, Wallace Stegner.

Of these, Wallace Stegner's career was at once the most normal and much the most distinctive. All four men were prolific writers, but in Stegner's work, both in fiction and nonfiction, there are definite peaks—*The Big Rock Candy Mountain, Beyond the Hundredth Meridian, Wolf Willow, Angle of Repose, Crossing to Safety,* the *Collected Stories.* Fisher and Manfred, though both university men, were strange, in some ways isolate, figures, scribbling on and on, their voices growing somehow fainter and fainter even as they scribbled. They are interesting now mainly for the quirkiness of their efforts. Fisher's first book, and Manfred's last, were books of poems. Both were large men with Wolfeian ambitions. Fisher wrote a Wolfeian tetralogy; Manfred (whose real name was Feike Feikema, a Frisian name) a Wolfeian trilogy. Manfred invented a place called Siouxland, where many of his novels were set; Fisher took

91

on the whole history of mankind in a twelve-volume novel sequence, the *Testament of Man* series. Viewed nowadays, their works look as ragged as the vast region they tried to write about. They are never entirely uninteresting, but neither are they compelling.

Wright Morris is a perplexing example of a first-rate sensibility who never quite produced a first-rate book—or if he has, it's his book of criticism, *The Territory Ahead.* Morris is also an excellent photographer; so good that from the first his photography has challenged his prose. His picture books *The Inhabitants, Land of the Free,* and *Love Affair: A Venetian Journal,* call one back, and his many novels do not.

Reflecting on these three careers, Fisher, Manfred, Morris, leads one to suspect that the frontier and postfrontier really offered more to the historian than it did to the novelist. In Nebraska Mari Sandoz, after much struggle and years of rejection, finally published her wonderful biography of her father, *Old Jules.* She moved east and went on to write well about the beaver men, the cattlemen, Crazy Horse, and in *Love Song to the Plains,* the Great Plains themselves.

In Oklahoma the historian Angie Debo, who lived to be ninety-eight, started out in a sodbuster's shack, overcame the early lack of educational opportunities, persevered, was awarded a doctorate in history, and went on to become the principal historian of what one might call the Second Dispossession of the Five Civilized Tribes. In three strong and somber histories—*The Rise and Fall of the Choctaw Republic, And Still the Waters Run,* and *The Road to Disappearance*—she describes in painstaking detail how the Five Tribes were chiseled and cheated out of the land in the West, theirs forever—or while the grass grows, the sun shines, and the waters run. At the age of eighty-six Angie Debo delivered a fine biography of Geronimo, who died at Fort Sill when she was nineteen years old.

One missed opportunity I myself particularly regret was the chance to take a class from Walter Prescott Webb, who came to Rice for a semester while I was in graduate school there. Webb was probably as able a student of the Western frontier as we have had; his writing far surpassed Frederick Jackson Turner's in scope. He came from Abilene, about one hundred miles south of where I grew up, and himself had early contact with the pioneer experience. Though nearly two generations separated me from Webb—he was old when I was young—we shared a sense of the frontier as being something that had only recently passed. Webb wrote one of the first thorough studies of the plains environment, focusing particularly on the determinative factor of aridity (*The Great Plains,* 1931). Later he broadened his inquiry and considered the Americas themselves as frontier (*The Great Frontier,* 1952).

That missed chance is still a faint line across my memory. I several times walked past the classroom where he was teaching. He kept the door open, but he spoke quietly and I cannot remember overhearing a single thing he said. At that time I was still frenziedly trying to educate myself in literary modernism. I knew that Webb was important, but did not anticipate someday becoming interested in the American frontier myself. There stood one of its greatest students, with his coat off and his shirtsleeves rolled up. But I never met him.

Nor did I meet J. Evetts Haley, who, despite his

deeply reactionary politics, was a brilliant historian and master of a considerably more graceful prose than Webb's —or J. Frank Dobie's, either. Haley's biography of Charles Goodnight remains the single best biography of a cattle-man—perhaps of a Western figure of any kind. That book is as good a place to start as any if one seeks to understand the attitudes and philosophies of the people such as my grandparents who settled the west Texas frontier.

J. Evetts Haley, Walter Prescott Webb, and Angie Debo, all people I could not be bothered to read when I was young, I refer to often now, as I have at last grasped that the task of understanding where one came from and *how* one came from it are not as simple as I would have supposed it to be when I was younger.

Then, of course, I was involved in an act of escape: the escape from the cowboy life, the life of men and horses, into the culture of books. In fact, I *read* my way out of that culture, and now, in my seventh decade, have been catching up on a few of the writers who read *their* way out before me.

Webb did, Dobie did, but Haley didn't—not to the same extent or in the same way. J. Evetts Haley remained a rancher-historian to the end of his life.

READING

1

◌ I WAS six years old when my cousin brought me the nineteen boys' books—all of them were common boys' books of the twenties and thirties, most published by the illustrious firm of Grosset and Dunlap, a firm that published photoplay editions and cheap reprints of popular books. In the box of nineteen books were such page-turners as *Poppy Ott and the Stuttering Parrot* and *Jerry Todd and the Whispering Cave*. Though I had passed the first grade it was only in theory that I could read, because, until Cousin Bob arrived with his box, I had nothing *to* read. As it happened, the first book I actually plucked out of the box and opened was a stirring tale of adventure among the Canadian Mounties called *Sergeant Silk, the Prairie Scout*—I was amazed to discover that in fact I *could* read. I proceeded to read it right straight through, marveling at the resourcefulness of Sergeant Silk. Fifty years later, spotting a copy in a bookshop in Tucson, I reacquired it, for old times' sake.

By the time I had read my way through that box of nineteen books I knew I had found something important—indeed, something central: a pleasure whose stability I could always depend on. With the exception of one confusing period, though many individual books have failed to hold me, reading itself has remained the constant pleasure I immediately found it to be.

Fortunately, by the time I had read those nineteen boys' books three or four times apiece, we had moved into town and acquired *My Book House* and *The World Book*. Those two compendious sets occupied me until the next big event in my reading life, which was the arrival of the first paperbacks on a rack in the local drugstore. Thanks to that paperback rack I was among the first to applaud Mickey Spillane, not because of his writing but because of the famous cleavage cover of *I, the Jury*—that cover, which helped the book sell many millions of copies, could stand for an era, paperbackwise.

In those years I was happy to grab anything from Kathleen Winsor *(Forever Amber)* to Erskine Caldwell. Sometime in early adolescence I somehow derived the confused notion that Eastern religious texts were actually treasures of eroticism. Perhaps I confused some vague mention of the *Kama Sutra* with an equally vague mention of the *Bhagavad Gita*, a work I pored over at length without being able to find a single sexy part.

One thing was certain: the paperbacks available in the drugstore were much more interesting than anything I was being asked to read in school. Even at the long-awaited senior level we were offered nothing more advanced than Longfellow, Bryant, and Sidney Lanier. The fiction was apt to be Poe, O. Henry, Bret Harte, or at best, Hawthorne. The teachers were not above making us do book reports on Riley, Whittier, and the dog stories of Albert Payson Terhune. Had I been forced to find my way to literature via high school instruction I would probably have stopped somewhere around "The Lady or the Tiger?"

Fortunately, there were the excitements of the drugstore, and they *were* excitements. I went in almost every day, to see what new paperbacks had arrived. In later years, too broke to scout real bookshops, I began to reac-

quaint myself with the early publications of the first successful paperback houses: Pocket Books, Bantam, Avon,
Dell, Popular Library, and Gold Medal. An assiduous scout,
I soon recovered many of the titles I had first purchased in
the Archer City drugstore, in the late forties and early
fifties.

What got skipped, in my drugstore education, was
the whole curve of literary modernism. When I began
much later to reacquire early paperbacks I was surprised
to find Faulkner and Hemingway, Virginia Woolf and D. H.
Lawrence among them. My first clue that any such people
existed was a Mentor book which I picked up casually in
1954: *Highlights of Modern Literature,* a collection of essays from the *New York Times Book Review* edited by
Francis Brown. I had never heard of Francis Brown, or the
New York Times either, but that paperback, which sold for
thirty-five cents, had essays either by or on Auden, Orwell,
Frost, Hemingway, Thomas Mann, Yeats, Faulkner, Gide,
V. S. Pritchett, Joyce Cary, E. M. Forster, and Virginia
Woolf.

Had it not been for that lone paperback I would have
arrived at Rice in the fall of 1954 never having heard of
Ernest Hemingway, T. S. Eliot, Faulkner, Pound, or any of
the other high moderns. My first glimpse of Hemingway
probably came when *Life* magazine put the Karsh portrait
on the cover. My knowledge of modern history was limited to what I could pick up listening to the radio, but
since I much preferred the serials to the news reports it
wasn't much. I knew nothing of communism and was puzzled for years as to exactly why General MacArthur got
fired. Where literature was concerned I knew, if I remember correctly, only one foreign name, Cervantes—a copy

of *Don Quixote* had somehow found its way into my hand. It's possible that I didn't yet grasp the difference between England and New England—at the time, in my reckoning, Shakespeare didn't count as a foreign name.

When I arrived at Rice my mind was about as close to being a tabula rasa as could be imagined. I was even ignorant of my own ignorance, and after all, was only eighteen—not knowing anything was nothing to be particularly embarrassed about. There was still time to read—if not everything, at least a lot.

Over the last forty-three years I have been doing just that. Although I had decent teachers I soon saw that—with one exception—I was reading more than they were. They had a big head start, but I was catching up. Literature, as I saw it then, was a vast open range, my equivalent of the cowboy's dream. I felt free as any nomad to roam where I pleased, amid the wild growth of books. Eventually I formed my own book herds and brought them into more or less orderly systems of pasturage. I even branded them with a bookplate that had once been the family brand: a stirrup drawn simply and elegantly by my father.

The teacher I wasn't outreading, and the one, consequently, whom I paid the most attention to, was the now mainly forgotten scholar of the eighteenth century Alan Dugald McKillop, a stooped and rather shuffling figure at Rice when I arrived. I never knew Alan McKillop well, but I respected him greatly. In my last year as a graduate student I took his course in the English novel—but it was not as a teacher that I was in awe of him: it was as a reader. I was just glad he was there, as an embodiment of learning of the old-school, unfrivolous kind. At Harvard he had been a pupil of Kittredge, Santayana, and William James.

For myself, just beginning to glimpse a few towers and turrets in the deep mist of knowledge, Alan McKillop represented a level of learning that (I came to believe) had existed only in Cambridge, Massachusetts, around 1910, when my father was just getting his three annual months of schooling in a one-room schoolhouse. As I listened to Alan McKillop I came to realize that if any man had really read the whole of English literature, from the Anglo-Saxon fragments to Anthony Powell, it was he. (At a tea in his home, the one time I was invited there, in 1959, he showed me Powell's books, and also those of C. P. Snow, whose academic novels he admired.)

Though not a particularly inspiring lecturer, Alan McKillop did leave one with the sense—valuable to me then—that literature, whether one wrote it, taught it, or just read it, could be a lifelong occupation; one could approach it in a leisurely way, to be sure, but one needed to approach it seriously.

With Dr. McKillop as an example I figured out that the way to find out what to read was to locate a great reader and follow in his or her tracks. There are, though, surprisingly few great readers—they are as rare now as giant pandas. Once one is located, even his obiter dicta are not to be disregarded. The next one I met personally was Susan Sontag, and that was thirty years after I studied with McKillop. Joe Alsop, politically 180 degrees to the right of Susan, was also a great reader, one I came to know just as his life was ending.

Most of the great readers whose tracks I've followed eagerly I never met, of course. I merely knew them through the reports—usually voluminous—that they made on what they read; their books, in other words. In college

the courses I found most useful were straightforward historical surveys. I wanted to know how history proceeded,
from prehistory until now, but I was never especially interested in literature courses. Where literature was concerned
I preferred from the first to go my own way, roving around
on the great open range. Though I was willing to listen to
what certain teachers had to say about a given book or
even a genre, my general attitude was a don't-fence-me-in
attitude. I soon came to know the Rice stacks as well as my
father knew his pastures.

Even when I had only the nineteen boys' books, the
first feeling I got from literature was a feeling of independence. In general I didn't feel the need of a professional
guide to this new country, though a little later, I was more
than willing to be guided by writers who wrote well about
what they had read. Several literary journalists of a now very
old-fashioned sort led me to books at first. Somewhere I
picked up a book by J. C. Squire, who for a time wrote a literary column under the name Solomon Eagle. A collection
of these columns, called *Books in General,* perfectly suited
my purpose. Books in general were exactly what I wanted
to know about. Having come from nowhere and read nothing, to me literary journalists were as Plato and Aristotle.
Saintsbury, Mencken, Huneker, Arnold Bennett, Pritchett,
Edmund Wilson, Kenneth Rexroth were—at varying
times—godsends to me because they mentioned books I
had never heard of, read, or seen. I remember vividly when
Edmund Wilson's literary chronicles began to be printed in
Anchor paperbacks. I went on, in time, to read more
sophisticated literary criticism, or critical theory, but on the
whole with less enjoyment than I received from the meat-
and-potatoes literary reporters. I still go through critical

books, but at a brush-popping pace—I'm less interested in explication than I am in hearing about books or authors I haven't read.

I'm sure that the essential privacy of the act of reading was for me always part of its force. My first reading was unshared. Though ranches are supposed to consist mostly of wide open spaces, in fact much ranch work is communal. We were always borrowing cowboys from one small ranch and lending our own labor to another. And if there weren't cowboys around there would usually be a vet, or a horseshoer, or a county agent, or a man to fix the windmill, or another cattleman who had stopped by to seek my father's advice. In my teenage years I grew bolder about reading during gaps in the work. I can't recall that anyone ever asked me what I was reading and I never volunteered a word about it.

I think my strong sense of reading as a private thing was one reason I made an indifferent teacher. I wanted to read, not talk about it. One of the valuable things I did do was compose a reading list of my own off-the-beaten-track enthusiasms, interesting books I had come across that I felt sure no other teacher would be likely to recommend.

But the problem with reading lists, even one as intelligent as Cyril Connolly's *The Modern Movement*, is that they are all in a sense dead letters, guides for the unadventurous, those without the time or the ambition to hunt around and make discoveries for themselves. The great readers will always know about books that neither the marketplace nor the academy has got around to.

I quickly began to need books as naturally as I need food. The minute I began to write I felt a tension between reading and writing that, instead of abating, has grown more intense with the shortening of my life's horizon. I'm now in my sixties, which means that I'm looking at a maximum of about thirty more years of life. Which should I do? Read, or write? Though I have now read a lot of books the range is still green with thousands of potentially interesting books yet unread. It's been with constant—if low-grade—reluctance that I've taken time off from reading in order to write fiction, screenplays, essays, and the like. So far I've kept the two activities in uneasy balance, gotten away with doing both, but keeping that balance may not be possible much longer. I have, in any case, the feeling that I've already overgrazed the plains of fiction; the grasshoppers of time have stripped most of that foliage.

There is not much of a record, in the memoirs of writers, about the tension I have just described, the silent competition between reading and writing. I don't know if many writers feel it. I do know that some writers seem to resent reading, to resent literature even—as if it were unfair competition. Henry Miller has written a fine celebration of reading, *The Books in My Life,* but in this he is unusual. On the rare occasions when I visit another writer's home I always immediately look at their books, which in too many cases consist mainly, if not exclusively, of books they've been sent to blurb or perhaps review. Victorian, Edwardian, even early-twentieth-century English writers (and French) were commonly photographed in their libraries, in front of their bookcases, which were not only well ordered but full. Few writers now seem to have large libraries, deliberately and selectively acquired. Most merely have accumulations of books which somehow got into their houses, toward which they display little interest or affection. What happened? Why is it that the well-stocked libraries in which tolerant parents encouraged their intellectually curious children to browse hardly exist anymore?

As a bookseller in Washington, D.C., I've purchased a number of such libraries, most of them founded on solid Arnoldian sentiments: that is, the belief that an educated, progressive household ought to contain a substantial portion of the best that has been thought and said. Of course, Arnold's opinions applied mainly to the educated middle class. The upper class had sport and the lower class misery. These libraries were not cut to any strict mold—the standard sets might be there, but so would a large mélange, or miscellany, reflecting the owner's curiosity. They were often quite catholic in taste and enabled many a young woman—Virginia Woolf, for example—to derive a decent education, if they applied themselves.

What I'm wondering—to drift back to my original intention, which was to investigate stories—is whether this level of curiosity exists today and what is feeding it if it does exist. Benjamin posits curiosity—he assumes that all people are naturally curious about the experience of others, and considers such curiosity to be highly practical: if pursued, it should help people live better lives. In his view curiosity, through much of human time, had been nurtured to some extent by boredom. Wandering seamen or traveling artisans with stories to tell didn't happen by every day. When one showed up he would have an audience already primed.

Who is bored, in Western society, in quite that way today? It may be true that much of the society suffers from an essential boredom, but boredom is apt to lie deep in the psyche, well muffled by the buzz from the television set.

Perhaps if the buzz could be silenced people would still be willing to sit down and listen to a good story, but we'll never know because the buzz is never likely to be silenced. There will always, now, be twenty-four-hour news, twenty-four-hour weather, an endless ribbon of information feeding into our lives. Real curiosity now gets little chance to develop—it's smothered with information before it can draw a natural breath.

The popularity and wide dissemination of the personal computer would, I imagine, induce a deep melancholia in Walter Benjamin, even if he were happy with his own PC. He, after all, held the view that information was the enemy of story. We now live in a world in which the sum total of accumulated human knowledge—plus any of its parts—can be accessible within a few minutes, or even a few seconds. Most of the world's great dictionaries and encyclopedias are on CD-ROM, and the combined image riches of the world's great museums will soon be similarly stored.

Everywhere that's on-line, which is almost everywhere, lore is being replaced by fact. My grandson is interested in snakes. He knows that the Gabon viper is probably the most poisonous snake in the world, with some of the more dangerous Australian snakes close seconds. He knows this because he has a comprehensive dictionary of reptiles, but also he's seen these snakes and many other animals on the Discovery Channel. He is rather casual about the Gabon viper, in fact, because all the authorities have assured him that it's a shy, timid creature. The lore has been drained out, the snake demystified, because however potent its poison, the mystery has been drained out. The kind of elemental wonder that refreshes one's hopes for the race can now mainly be found in children too young to have mastered the TV remote. Even the rancorous claims of family life can rarely distract them from their engagement with the media.

I doubt that this is a bad thing—family life, after all, has a way of dissolving into a number of often-repeated set pieces. Also, I personally distrust nostalgia for times when, supposedly, life was simpler and less confusing. I lived through quite a few decades of those simpler times and remember them as containing less confusion but also less stimulation. It may be that thanks to TV and the Internet life is being lived more indirectly—Woody Allen did once refer to his own life as a distraction—but this may not be particularly bad. Perhaps E-mail will resurrect the letter from the early grave that was dug for it by the telephone. Perhaps stories will find new routes to listeners, arrive in new forms.

The hunger for information is, after all, normal, but the need for continuity may be even stronger. Renata Adler has written cogently about the force of soap opera in her (our) life, pointing out that the soaps are what we have now in place of long relationships and family continuities. Some soaps have gone on for more than twenty years, far longer than the average marriage. Something of the same is true of the more successful sitcoms, from *The Honeymooners* and *I Love Lucy* through *The Mary Tyler Moore Show, All in the Family, The Bob Newhart Show,* and more recently, *Cheers, Murphy Brown, Roseanne,* and *Seinfeld.*

I note in my own family, which has had its ups and downs, its deaths and discontinuities, a strong interest still in family stories. I've come to recognize that one of the functions of a grandparent or family elder is to pass on these stories, in an effort to sustain a sense of family history across time and the many separations that occur. This is an important function—the forces that blow families apart have reached gale force in our time. One can see this in the demise of the family dinner table. In my childhood it was uncommon for the family to eat less than two meals a day around the same kitchen table. (We ate in the dining room only on state occasions: Christmas, Thanksgiving, or if the preacher came home for Sunday lunch.) Since my father breakfasted at four-thirty or five in the morning, we children were not expected to breakfast with him, though my mother was. He usually came in from the pastures for lunch unless the work of the day could not be interrupted, in which case my mother took lunch to the cowboys, wherever they were.

But dinner (called supper then) was a virtually inviolable ritual. Only natural disasters, severe weather, or some catastrophic breakdown in the day's work schedule could delay or abrogate family dinners at the kitchen table. In this I don't believe we were exceptional. There was no fast food in the forties and little in the fifties. The first drive-in, precursor of the Dairy Queen, appeared in Archer City while I was in high school. Working- and middle-class families sat down at the dinner table every night—the shared meal was the touchstone of good manners. Indeed, that dinner table was the one time when we were all together, every day: parents, grandparents, children, siblings. Rudeness between siblings, or a failure to observe the etiquette of passing dishes to one another, accompanied by "please" and "thank you," was the training ground of behavior, the place where manners began.

There was then a family circle of sorts, and now it's

been broken. Families are more and more likely to eat at disparate hours, if they eat in the same house at all, and often, if they *are* in the same house, eat facing the television, rather than one another—they eat, that is, in the glow of the evil eye, an eye indifferent to and discouraging of conversation or anything resembling good manners. Once daily attention is withdrawn, even for the short time it takes most people to eat supper, family interaction is diminished and as often as not lost entirely. Family members miss a daily chance to catch up with one another—they end up responding to the characters in *Roseanne* or *Cheers* rather than to their own parents or siblings.

For the past several centuries the bonding power of the family dinner table has been one of the few constants, and now it's binding no more. The potency of the media is now stronger than that of the family. The wonder is that families still exist at all, since the forces of modern life mainly all pull people away from a family-centered way of life.

It would be interesting if an anthropologist with the smarts of a Lévi-Strauss would apply them to our current behavior with food and food rituals, such as they are. If one considers such rituals from the Depression until now, one might conclude that it's among the leisured, old-money rich that the habits of dining have changed least. For the old rich, dinner is still a form of entertainment, an important social ritual. They eat late, after a leisurely cocktail hour; a few even still dress for dinner. Their patterns were always Anglophilic, and remain so.

The middle and working classes normally ate supper at the end of the working day, which would have been long. If one breakfasts at 5 A.M., as is still common in ranching families, dinner at 5 or 6 P.M. comes none too soon. Though there may be a certain amount of general conversation—weather, "Good roast," report cards, "Can I have the car Friday night?"—these meals are rarely leisurely. All the food is put on the table at once (rather than course by course, as with the rich) and more is shoveled into the serving dishes as needed. The notions of a progression of courses—salad, entree, dessert—was unknown, though there might have been a certain amount of place clearing before dessert, in order to make room for pie plates, cobbler, and the like. Meals were practical occasions; necessary fuel was taken in; people ate to get full. There was a modest order of precedence: the father and breadwinner would be served first, unless a preacher was present. Preachers took precedence over fathers. There might be a modest amount of squabbling over who got the best piece of chicken—the wishbone—but not much. Preachers were most likely to appear at Sunday lunch; having just sweated himself down delivering a fiery sermon, he would be allowed to serve himself first. The children came last— the classic expression of their problem is Governor Jimmy Davis's poignant ballad "Take an Old Cold Tater and Wait."

The food itself was never adventurous; the meats were round steak, pot roast, or fried chicken. Pork might occasionally be served to the family, but never to company. The most exotic dish I can recall from my whole childhood was Jell-O salad.

It took television only one long generation to destroy the family dinner table; where, when, and how someone ate came to be determined by what there was to watch. The order of precedence migrated: who got the best piece of chicken came to be less important than who got to choose which program to watch. Siblings fought more bitterly over program choice than they ever had over food. Then someone invented the TV dinner—after which it became rarer and rarer for a whole family to gather round the old kitchen table—someone might occasionally eat a bowl of cereal at it, but the family would be elsewhere.

And of course, the fact was that even in the heyday of family dining not all mothers were good and enthusiastic cooks. Frozen dinners soon became competitive. The father was most apt to grumble about this, pushing for the survival of home cooking long after the rest of the family had pretty much forgotten what home cooking was. Why should Mom or Sister have to peel potatoes when there was a McDonald's right down the street? What Dad may have noticed, once he no longer automatically took his place at the head of the dinner table, as was his right as the head of the family, was that he no longer *was* the head of the family. His place had been taken by Walter Cronkite, who, even more than the president, became unofficial head of the national family for a while—insofar as the national family had a head.

The old bonding power of the family dinner table was lost as the center of the family life gradually shifted from the kitchen to wherever the TV was; female energies shifted too, from the preparation of food and the cleaning up that took place after a meal to just being sure that the freezer was stocked with plenty of frozen pizza.

No sooner had the television set become a commonplace in American homes than the parents began to be apprehensive about its effects. "We never eat together anymore" became a common lament, sounded often by parents who must have sensed that something valuable—

they may not have been quite sure what—was going away or being lost. As the children grew into teenagers it became rarer and yet more rare to see them in the house at mealtimes; and then the very concept of mealtime began to lose its force. What is mealtime now, in America? It's become a meaningless concept.

Food itself, once little of it was cooked at home, assumed an ever more severe practicality. It became harder and harder to maintain a distinction between fast-food restaurants and filling stations. Exxon, Chevron, Shell, and the like were filling stations for your cars, whereas, to about the same degree, McDonald's, Burger King, and Taco Bell became filling stations for your bodies. When these competitive entities are working at full efficiency it takes only a little longer to fill your body than it does to fill your car.

Indeed, the food itself may soon become less important than the speed of delivery. Instead of eating to store up energy for tomorrow's work, people eat—or at least, kids eat—to store up energy for tonight's leisure.

After a generation or two during which food quality and eating standards had steadily declined, and in which the old practice of partaking of food together as a form of family bonding had virtually disappeared, food began to make a comeback, not, however, because it tasted good or was a pleasure to eat, but as a form, I believe, of theology. Food came back to save you, packaged now by the health food industry, whose orthodoxies are as strict as those of any faith. First and foremost, fat—or Satan—had to be driven out. (Visit a supermarket in Brentwood, Santa Monica, or Beverly Hills, California, and you will soon see how successful this crusade has been: you can walk until you drop without seeing any food that will admit to having fat in it.) Food that was just plain good gave way to food that was good for you. The suggestion that fat-free food will save you from death—perhaps not forever but certainly for a long time—is everywhere present in supermarkets, most of which are kept spotless, with uniformed security guards in the parking lots to turn away the homeless, that is, the conspicuously unsaved. The supermarkets themselves are more and more like churches—a few even have holistic therapies available for those whose spiritual life needs immediate attention. Buying a pound of bacon in one of these stores will usually draw frowns: you will reveal yourself to be an apostate. One has to try hard to take the long view at such times, to remember that health food orthodoxies don't really do as much harm as religious orthodoxies. Perhaps, in the end, they are only curiosities, like the tulip mania that seized the Dutch people in the seventeenth century.

2

THE FIRST book I read that belonged indubitably to world literature was *Don Quixote.* How I came by it, or exactly when, or what edition I read, I cannot now remember. Probably I was about thirteen, a ranch boy who had never had a really good book to read before. (Not everyone agrees that it is a great book: Edmund Wilson, an admitted Iberophobe, thought it a bore and said as much to Harry Levin, prompting that scholar's classic rejoinder, "Harvard disagrees.")

It is clear that Edmund Wilson, a Princeton man, didn't give a shit whether Harvard disagreed or not. Mario Praz also had his problems with Iberian culture, though I don't recall that he particularly disliked Cervantes, as Edmund Wilson did.

For myself, stumbling on *Don Quixote* was a profound experience, although I could not have said why at the time. I just knew that *Don Quixote* was different in kind from *Sergeant Silk, the Prairie Scout* or *Poppy Ott and the Stuttering Parrot.* Oddly, since I have a book scout's visual memory of almost every book I've seen, I have no memory at all of what my first *Don Quixote* looked like, though I do remember my second copy, a Modern Library Giant, purchased at around age eighteen. All I can remember about my first reading is that I did it in the loft of the barn, a place I often retreated to to read, partly because of the privacy, partly because I enjoyed being high up, where I could look north and south and see the whole ranch. Although poultry had largely ceased to be a threat by that time, I still liked to climb above their cacophony when possible.

From the loft of the barn, or from the little platform on top of the windmill, I could look north into the Great Plains and do some serious daydreaming. Probably one of the reasons for my immediate identification with Don Quixote and Sancho was that they went horseback across a plain. Also, at least in the first part, their misadventures often involved animals, as mine did. Horses were always kicking them, a danger one had to prepare for if one has horses around. I could readily identify with the landscape, with the two men's mode of travel. They were clearly in sheep country, not cattle country, but not being a real cowboy, I was never able to acquire the prejudice against sheep that many cattlemen have. (In Archer County there were then no sheep to be prejudiced against.) Also, we had a windmill, and I could readily understand how someone who was a little deranged might mistake it for a giant.

Moving down yet one more level of the story, I also responded to the classic opposition of types, Don Quixote and Sancho Panza, the visionary and the practical man; in this pairing I soon gave my loyalty to Sancho. I felt like the practical man myself, in constant conflict with visionaries—or at least one visionary, my keeper, my Jeeves, my constant companion, the elderly cowboy Jesse Brewer.

Jesse was not, strictly speaking, even a cowboy; I'm not sure what he had done with himself during the eighty years that preceded our acquaintance. He had survived, that's all, and now was being superannuated. His job with us was to be in effect a mounted baby-sitter. The cowboys, with serious work to do, could not slow themselves to the snail-like pace of my detestable pony: ergo, Jesse. He was the age of my grandmother but made of considerably less stern stuff. My grandmother was unshakable, whereas Jesse was easily, constantly shaken. He struck me from the first as insanely fearful, a condition my mother also suffered from. No situation could be so placid, so unthreatening, so safe, but that Jesse—like the Don—could find catastrophe lurking in it. Riding over a level plain he would imagine that both our mounts would step in holes at the same time: they would stumble, throw us, perhaps fall on us. No bush was so insignificant that it might not harbor a rattlesnake. If I wanted to wade in a pond, Jesse would immediately suspect the pond of being aboil with water moccasins, or snapping turtles, or gars. Our hill, if you

copy was an abridgment, or even a modernization, so that I just didn't feel that these events were happening in another century. But it really didn't seem old—no older than a number of the cowboys who were then still around. The Don was no crazier than Jesse, Sancho no more put upon than I was myself. The narrative connected not only with what I saw but with what I had been told about cowboys of yore. There, to the south, was the spring where the great herds had watered. Don Quixote would no doubt have suspected the cattle of being Saracens in disguise, a confusion I could understand. The Don was also a little like my Uncle Johnny, who led a colorful life ranching near Muleshoe. Uncle Johnny traveled more than his siblings; he was the family's wandering seaman—he told many stories. Also—like the Don—he was accident-prone and was constantly being injured by his own livestock.

It may be that the reason *Don Quixote* seemed neither old nor foreign to me when I first read it is that so much of it is a country story, a story of open places. Later, though, when I had stopped being a country person, my rereading of *Don Quixote* was colored by my experience as a rare-book man. The old Don was clearly a bibliomaniac, the first in literature, collecting those romances of chivalry. He seemed crazy in the way many book collectors are crazy. I've now had the opportunity to observe many collectors, some of them prominent, and there's something of the old Don in most of them. There are, of course, sober, practical men who collect books, but most of the really interesting book people I've known, whether dealers, scouts, or collectors, have mainly been a little mad.

3

◌ SO LOCKED was I into the geography of our hill and our life on the plains that, even when I approached college age, I didn't really envision leaving it. Most of our pastures consisted of rolling country—from the rises and ridges of all of them I could see Archer City. It was a little like being a farm laborer in a Hardy novel, with Archer County as my Wessex. The village, or manor, where we returned every night was never long out of sight.

The hold the landscape had on me was so powerful that I couldn't really imagine living long in any other. I assumed that, after college, I would return, peasantlike, to my life in sight of the Windthorst church and the Archer City water tower, that I would live always in sight of those little clumps of buildings on the plain. No other place had yet managed to engage my imagination, because I had been no other place. How I would make a living, with our already limited acreage and the cattle business dying, was a matter I didn't dwell on.

I was largely satisfied with my life and with our quasi-rural culture, except for one thing: books. The tiny high school library yielded little. Wichita Falls's one bookstore yielded little more, though it did contain, near the rear, a few shelves of Modern Library books. I bought my first copy of *Madame Bovary* there, in the old translation by Eleanor Marx Aveling. In those days the Modern Library printed its backlist on the verso of the dust wrapper. That list was to me a kind of Aladdin's cave, only I didn't know what the password was. One sign of things to come was that from the beginning I sought to *acquire* books. I could, I suppose, have secured a library card to the public library in Wichita Falls, but I didn't want books I had to bring back. I wanted books to keep, books that I could *consider*—think about for a few days before I read them. My approach to most books was slow—I might seize them quickly but wait awhile to read them. *War and Peace,* for example, which I also bought in a Modern Library Giant. I kept it around, looked at it, puzzled over the names, dipped in here and there, a process that went on for perhaps a year before I sat down and read the book.

From the first I was attracted to the look and feel of books—I liked to enter what Walter Benjamin called the aura of reading, which involved mental preparation and was a way, I guess, of savoring the experience ahead. This time of anticipation is one of the pleasures of having a personal library.

I learned early that the kink in my attachment to Archer County, and to west Texas in general, was that the place was bookless. This problem kept me elsewhere for thirty or so years of my life but I solved it eventually by bringing about a quarter of a million books to this little town, twenty thousand of my own and another two hundred thousand or so in the bookshops that I opened here.

Just beyond our little hay field, on the south edge of Archer City, stood the town's most imposing house, the home of an oilman named Will Taylor. In its day (the late twenties) the house must have seemed a mansion, but it was really just a large, commodious, prairie-style house. (I now own it and live in it, with my twenty thousand books.) Mr. Will Taylor was a very successful and rather refined oilman who had suffered a crippling tragedy. He lost his only child, a son, in an oil field accident. His boy dead, Mr. Taylor withdrew from business and took to reading. In the late afternoon he would drive to town in his Packard limousine and get the mail. The light in his second-floor study burned all night—from my small bedroom in our garage I could look across the hay field and see that light. Mr. Taylor and I were the only two people in Archer City who liked to read all night—only a hay field separated us, but I cannot remember meeting him more than once or twice.

In a gully below his house was a dump which I liked to poke around in once in a while, curious about what a rich man would throw away. One day I came across several bundles of discarded book catalogues, neatly tied with string. They were catalogues from the distinguished English firm of Frances Edwards Ltd, the once excellent shop in Marylebone High Street—I believe it was the only building in London built specifically to be a bookshop. The firm of Frances Edwards issued more than one thousand catalogues before it failed.

The twenty-five or thirty catalogues in Mr. Taylor's dump opened for me the long-hidden entrance to Aladdin's cave—in my case the world of antiquarian books and the people who sell them, who hunt them, who collect them. Quite a few years later, as a bookseller, I went to Marylebone High Street and bought books from Frances Edwards.

When I bought Mr. Taylor's house in 1986 I was surprised to find that there were only a few bookcases in it. Perhaps he was a slow reader—or perhaps he scarcely read at all. Broken by the loss of his son, he may only have sat and grieved. It was nonetheless a satisfaction to me to put several of the books I bought at Frances Edwards in the 1970s into Mr. Taylor's house. Very likely, over the years, I bought more books from them than he did; what is interesting is that in this small Texas town a firm of London booksellers had at least two customers.

4

◌ THE SUBTITLE of this essay, as many will have noticed, echoes Edmund Wilson's subtitle to his book *A Piece of My Mind,* his crotchety, old-fartish assembly of gripes and complaints about the deteriorating quality of American life. Fretful and petulant as that book is, it remains, like all Wilson's nonfiction prose, intensely readable. Most of Edmund Wilson's huge body of criticism consists essentially of high-level book reports; almost all of it remains readable, whether he is reporting on new books, old books, or the countries and times in which the books were written. He was a great reader who lived by commenting on his reading. Mencken's bite was sharper, but Wilson's reading was vast. Busy as Edmund Wilson was as a journalist, husband, father, seducer, and amateur magician, one comes away from that long, mostly uniform row of literary chronicles feeling that the center of his life was reading. His sexual appetites required frequent attention, but his literary appetite was insatiable—as it is with all great readers.

Coleridge, I suppose, was the grandparent of this type of great reader, but more typical models were Saintsbury in England and Sainte-Beuve in France. I realized long ago that I owe most of what education I have to a gallery of great readers, those who know early that there is never going to be time to read all there is to read, but do their darnedest anyway. Three great readers I have had the good fortune to know personally: Alan McKillop, Susan Sontag, and Joseph Alsop—it is impossible to imagine any of their lives if reading were to be subtracted from them. Other great readers whom I can track only through their reporting would be George Saintsbury (I read him before I realized he was supposed to be out of fashion), Virginia Woolf, V. S. Pritchett, the now nearly forgotten Paul Elmer More, Kenneth Rexroth, Stanley Edgar Hyman, and the multilingual George Steiner, whom I prefer in his high-journalistic rather than his incantatory mode.

John Updike I hardly know how to count. He is without question a great belletrist, and as good a spot reviewer as we have ever had, but it is hard to know, as one contemplates the mountain of those brilliant reviews—the latest collection, *Odd Jobs,* is so heavy one needs to keep a forklift by the bed just to lift it—what John Updike reads that he isn't paid to read. With someone like Pritchett one feels that he would have read the book whether he was being paid to review it or not. In that, Pritchett was like Wilson, though of course both of them made most of their living writing about books. Updike's impulses as a reader are harder to discern, though now and then, as in his great consideration of Emerson, one feels the subject carrying him deeper and deeper, farther from shore than he perhaps initially meant to swim.

One has to be grateful for those massed reviews, though—I read through them frequently, hoping to hear about books that might otherwise slip by.

The descendants of the great readers I have mentioned are too often merely fluent know-it-alls, of whom Christopher Hitchens might be considered the exemplar. There he is, every week or month, in the *Nation, Vanity Fair,* the *London Review of Books,* writing about history, politics, books, public figures, virtually anything that comes down the freeways of our global culture. I personally have seen Christopher Hitchens in public debate while so weary or drunk or both that he can hardly have known whether he was even facing his audience, or whether there *was* an audience—and yet not a detail of his argument was dropped and not any of his long and well-turned sentences were slurred. His speech, like his writing, is precise, often brilliant, sometimes spellbinding, rarely inelegant; and yet one feels—as with many of his high-journalistic peers—that all this knowledge (or at least all this information) is not really reading-derived, but has been acquired more or less by osmosis, by rubbing elbows with his journalistic peers in Washington, London, New York, Paris, Delhi, Tehran, or wherever. I might note that this fluency is something few Americans seem to possess; perhaps it stems from admirable European secondary education. I might note too that it is mainly those high journalists who seem to command the steadily released energies of their Victorian counterparts: Bagehot, Macaulay, Saintsbury.

The last-named critic, George Saintsbury, seems to have written about as much as he read, and he read an enormous amount. I have most of his books and they cover a wall—several of them are multivolume studies that are longer than the longest three-decker novel. In Saintsbury there seemed to be no tension between reading and writing; but if we move along to V. S. Pritchett, who was a fine short-story writer, one can occasionally sense the author being whipsawed back and forth between the essay-review and the short story or novel; the former had to be done to support the latter.

I've recently begun to form a small collection of the published table talk of various men of letters. It's now a neglected thing, table talk: Johnson had Boswell, Goethe had Eckermann, but nobody, so far as I know, is following Saul Bellow around taking down his off-the-cuff remarks; and for all that has been written about her and her circle, Virginia Woolf had to record most of her own comments and opinions.

One would be grateful for a volume of her table talk, hers and others; though Virginia Woolf reviewed widely, some great readers *don't* write book reports. It's likely to be at table, if at all, that they talk about their reading. Joe Alsop was one such, a political reporter who spent thirty-five years re-creating himself as an art historian, with some—but not complete—success. Joe Alsop prided himself on his food and his guests, but I thought that on the whole his books were more impressive—about twelve thousand well-selected and well-read books. Though Joe led an active, even hyperactive, social life and was eager to keep up with both local gossip and world affairs, I felt that—as with other great readers—reading was really the central activity of his life. To the end, like the others, he was driven by the same pulsing curiosity to read and then read more.

Susan Sontag is a reader who can almost be said to sweat literature—it is in her juices, as basketball is in Michael Jordan's. With Susan, I think, the tug of literature is as constant as breath. A characteristic she shares with all great readers is that, however stern she may intend to be, politically or philosophically, when she begins to talk about her reading she reveals a broadly catholic taste. The thrill Susan experiences when she spots a desired book she has not been able to find is probably comparable to that of a bird-watcher who at last glimpses a long-sought species.

5

MOST COMMITTED, lifelong readers find that at some point their interests undergo tectonic shifts. Until the age of thirty I was an avid reader of fiction. Under the aegis of Alan McKillop and one or two other professors, I luckily acquired the sense that I ought to know as much as possible about the history and the potentialities of this genre—the novel—that I was attempting to work in.

As a writer my love, first and last, has been the novel, and as a reader, the same is true. Though I admire much of the fine work that's been done in the short story, I seem, from the first, to have wanted that sense of a world that is to be found mainly in the novel, and especially in the great novels and novel systems of the nineteenth century: the worlds of Balzac, George Eliot, Dickens, Hardy, Thackeray, Gogol, Dostoyevsky, Flaubert, Tolstoy. The only American novelist who gave me a sense of a world on a comparable scale was Faulkner. Hemingway was not a world maker on that scale, nor were most of the nineteenth-century American writers. Melville does it in one book only—*Moby-*

Dick—and Henry James, great writer though he was, with his clashes of manners and mentalities, doesn't produce quite such a sense of a world as did the great Europeans. James did make worlds, but they were not worlds that—starting from Archer City—I could enter easily, whereas Faulkner was familiar, perhaps because he wrote about the South, a place I recognized but didn't like. For a time I associated the South only with misery—my misery—because I several times rode buses across it, in the process of a courtship, and the buses seemed always to arrive in either Tupelo, Mississippi, or Montgomery, Alabama, at three o'clock in the morning: modest dark nights of the South, perhaps, but memorable. I saw the South as a place of vainglory, bitterness, and megalomania, a place that, spiritually, was still devastated by its defeat in the Civil War to such a degree that it was, in a sense, all past: the opposite of Archer County, which was all present.

My elderly relatives, when I was young, were still bitter about Sherman—they talked as if he had marched through Georgia yesterday. This defining defeat and the society that succeeded it provided Faulkner with a tragic, authentic, and inexhaustible subject. The splendor of his themes and of much of his language affected me deeply, even if it was a little too close to home. I had in my life various poor-white relatives who were fully Southern in temperament.

Fortunately there was the great banquet of the European novel for me to feast at for many happy years. I spent most of my time with the English, the Russians, and the French—I still have trouble with the Germans. I not only read the novels, I read the biographies of the novelists and a fair amount of scholarship and theory about the novel. I was in graduate school at a time when Lukács was just being translated, when Wayne Booth, Northrop Frye, Dorothy Van Ghent, R. P. Blackmur, Leavis, Ian Watt, and others all had things to say about the novel and were saying them eloquently. I liked particularly the practical criticism, Pritchett's *The Living Novel* and Frank O'Connor's *The Mirror in the Roadway.*

I taught for a while, mainly at Rice, but the time soon came when I ceased to enjoy talking about writing: I just wanted to do it, and it was at about this point that the balance of my reading shifted. I ceased to be a reader of fiction and became a reader of history, biography, anthropology, and travel literature. Reading fiction came to seem like a form of talking shop. At about this time I fell under the spell of *The Road to Xanadu,* John Livingston Lowes's wonderful study of the sources of "Kublai Khan" and "The Rime of the Ancient Mariner," a study that made me feel that it would be interesting to know what various writers had been reading when they wrote the books I admired most; or for that matter, what various writers read when they weren't writing at all. I had read that Hemingway had a lot of books, Faulkner few, Beckett fewer. Stanley Edgar Hyman was said to have 35,000, C. K. Ogden 80,000 (UCLA bought them), and Isaac Foot 120,000. As a bookseller I was twice in the home of James M. Cain and was surprised to see that he owned no fiction at all, except what he himself had written; what he had in the way of a library was just a large shelf containing many *Who's Who*s and other biographical dictionaries.

Nowadays the urge to know what various writers read—or at least, what books they *owned*—can be satisfied by visiting the several libraries that have made a partic-

ular effort to acquire writers' libraries. The University of
Texas has long made a practice of buying writers' libraries
when they can—and not merely their libraries, their book-
shelves and library furniture as well. In Austin one can see
Evelyn Waugh's library, shelved as he shelved it at Combe
Fleury. Virginia Woolf's books are there, as well as Comp-
ton Mackenzie's. The University of Tulsa has not copied
Texas in attempting to re-create the writer's writing environment, but they do have Edmund Wilson's library, and
Cyril Connolly's too—Connolly's is, on the whole, the
more interesting. Connolly was a collector, Wilson an ac-
cumulator, though it is likely that what rarities Wilson had
acquired through his long career as a reviewer had long
since been sucked away by the rare-book trade, as had the
famous copy of *Three Stories and Ten Poems* that Ernest
Hemingway inscribed to him.

There circulated, in the sixties, the legend that
Thomas Pynchon read only the *Encyclopaedia Brittanica;*
it was even said that much of the erudition in *V.* came out
of the N–O volume of that great work.

The admirable critic Louis Menand recently expressed dismay that Thomas Pynchon thinks *On the Road*
is a great novel. Well, possibly *On the Road* isn't a great
novel, but it did have a great effect, and Pynchon's opinion
has a context—that context being the deadly, New Criticism–dominated, quasiacademic tone of American fiction
as it was in the early fifties. The English faculties in that
time were filled with people who had been trained by the
New Critics, and the New Critics had never been particularly acute about or much interested in fiction. They
favored Jamesian obscurities and stressed a kind of formalism that, in fiction, is boring. Many young writers in the

fifties struggled to write heavy, symbol-laden fiction that no one, including themselves, was very interested in.

Kerouac blew that formalism away. *On the Road* was the catalytic book for a generation of American writers— my generation. Many of them would go beyond it, or even repudiate it, but its effect at the time was liberating to a degree hard to imagine now. But Thomas Pynchon, product of Cornell, remembers it, and so do I. I read several copies of that book ragged, drawn by the delight Kerouac took in America. Hosts of jalopies, no doubt, were driven to death in imitation of Jack and Neal, or Sal and Dean, as they were in the book. It brought an adventurous spirit and a different, less constipated prose back to American readers, a prose that at least partially captured the sheer speed of contemporary experience.

As Kerouac himself grew heavier and heavier with sorrow, and as the late, inferior books spewed out, I began to wish he would just quit. He had said what he had to say already, had freed our fiction from its formalistic self-consciousness: that was enough.

I never met Kerouac but I did, years later, meet Neal Cassady, and found little about him to like. Neal Cassady had no achievement to put beside the novels of Kerouac or the poetry of Allen Ginsberg; all he had was his vitality. He reminded me of certain cowboys I've known, men with a scrap or two of education who happen to be very capable in physical ways—they can ride any horse, fix any machine—but few of them ever bring their mental equipment up to the level of their physical abilities. So it was with Cassady.

It is easy to criticize the Beats, major and minor, for all manner of sloppiness—stylistic, political, social—but from the perspective of a graduate student in the late fifties, the Beats were like mountain men, or like Huck Finn, striking out for new territory; the dash they made for open country, post Eliot, post Brooks and Warren, post Ransom and Tate, post Frye, Wellek, Empson, Leavis, and the rest, played out in about five years, though Allen Ginsberg went on, Wordsworth-like, for another forty. Today, when criticism or what once would have been called criticism is so narcissistic, so self-referential, and so French, it is hard to remember the days when criticism, or the practice of humanistic letters, had such power and such influence. Nowadays this has broken down into a few cobra-and-mongoose battles, fought in the halls of a few institutions. In that older time, when, in Randall Jarrell's phrase, every swan wanted to become a duck, certain critics were the *T. rex*es of the literary jungle, though now much of their labored prose seems as quaint as Saintsbury's—and less passionate.

I do remember a time when the force of these critical eminences produced a split in my attention; the counterforce was of course the (then) young novelists: Mailer, Styron, Capote, Baldwin, Carson McCullers, Calder Willingham, Gore Vidal, Bellow, and, low and ill in Milledgeville, Flannery O'Connor. All these and more were to be found in *New World Writing,* a series published by Signet, and other magazines. By the time I left graduate school, doctorateless, in 1960, the new novelists had come to seem a lot more interesting than the old critics.

Being poor, the only way I had to get new books in my undergraduate days was to review them for newspapers. I started with the *Wichita Falls Times and Record News;* Professor (soon to be Senator) John Tower briefly reviewed for the same book page. The first book I reviewed was *Dr. Zhivago*—since, at the time, I had scarcely even heard of Russia, it made for an inauspicious beginning. I soon went on to review for papers in Houston, Washington, D.C., and elsewhere, writing, in essence, small book reports. I might have four hundred words in which to discuss five books—all I remember is the thrill of opening the packages of books when they came, seeing what wonders had been cast up on my doorstep.

RECENTLY, AFTER a lapse of some thirty-five years, I looked into Edmund Wilson's *A Piece of My Mind,* curious as to why I had happened to remember it—or its subtitle, at least—just as I was beginning this essay. What correspondence could there be between what Edmund Wilson—impatiently—said long ago and what I want to say now?

I think the correspondence I was looking for came at the very end of *A Piece of My Mind* (written, as is this essay, in the author's sixty-second year). Speaking of the Talcotts, founders of Talcottville, New York, Wilson says: "They made their own candles and nails and they spun the cloth for their clothes. . . ." And of his father:

> Indoors he would occupy himself with the inspection of his fishing tackle, or whittle sticks into slender canes. He would relax here, as I can relax, at home with his own singularity as with the village life, at home with the strangeness of this isolated house as well as the old America that it represents so solidly.

I don't know about the old America, but I do know that I experienced something of that same quality of relaxation when, in the late seventies, I purchased my grandparents' house from my mother and brother and began, again, to spend time on the customary, familial hill. I am often aware of how poor a pioneer I would have made; nonetheless, I'm grateful to have known pioneers and to have gained—as Edmund Wilson did about a place where the pioneering had been done a century earlier—a sense of what they were up against. I doubt that my grandparents made their own nails, but they probably did, for a time, make their own candles, and virtually everything else that they used or wore; and they did stare into the emptiness and start the slow and uncertain process of filling it in.

Once one has understood to some slight degree what settling America meant in terms of work, privation, effort, and gained some sense of what the pioneers did with their energies and their spirit, it is easy to understand why they didn't do art—art had to wait until the country had been subdued and made responsive enough that it could supply the basic human needs.

6

Ö I AM of the generation of American writers that stayed in school a little too long, and the reason we did is that there was, in the late fifties, no more compelling place to be. By school I mainly mean graduate school. The only war available in the fifties was the Korean conflict, to which most of us were not drawn and from which we were protected by our excellent grade-point averages. The New Journalism, so sexy and exciting, had not yet been born—its stars, Tom Wolfe, David Halberstam, Gay Talese, Marshall Frady, and the rest, were still writing the old journalism, as were thousands of other old journalists who never became stars. Convention ruled, computers hadn't arrived, corporate takeovers were rare. There seemed to be nothing more exciting to do than read. One of the best novels—I had almost said studies—of the period is Philip Roth's second book, *Letting Go,* which catches the musty, slightly mildewed quality of graduate school life better than any other.

It was a time in which students with vast literary ambition were living in garage apartments in Iowa City or Urbana, wondering what they would actually turn out to be. For me, it was mainly a way to keep reading, to remain in the atmosphere of books and learning rather than going back to the ranch.

I wrote two novels during my first year in graduate school and, as a result, landed at Stanford with a Stegner Fellowship in 1960, where I now and then saw Yvor Winters striding majestically across the Stanford campus, pipe in hand, a kind of Saint Paul of literature. It was not until nearly forty years later that I met his gifted wife, Janet Lewis, author of that haunting, beautiful novella *The Wife of Martin Guerre.*

Just as, at Rice, I had been fortunate enough to get to know a few of the Kittredge-era scholars, I was equally fortunate, at Stanford, to have Malcolm Cowley and Frank O'Connor as teachers. There is, for young writers, a motivating excitement in knowing men who had once seen

Shelley plain—or in Cowley's case, Hemingway and Faulkner. Gossip about the great does as much as anything else to pull young writers deeper into the great stream of literary endeavor—it gives them something to hold in their imaginations as they live in those grubby garage apartments, scratching out their first poems or fictions.

Malcolm Cowley, for most of the semester when he sat with us, did just that: sat with us. By then he was deaf as a post—or chose to appear to be—and as noncommittal as Buddha. Only now and then a glint in his eye might reveal that he derived some small amusement from our gamboling and competing. (That famous class contained Ken Kesey, Peter Beagle, the Australian novelist Christopher Koch, two Kentuckians, a Scot, a Canadian, a Texas millionaire—he was only auditing—and the striking Joanna Ostrow, who arrived in class each day accompanied by her two borzois—or were they Afghans?)

Frank O'Connor, who showed up and dealt with us for the second semester, was far from being as noncommittal as Buddha; instead he brought some of the passions of the Irish Rebellion into our modest classroom. Occasionally he would be brought to tears by the folly of our sentiments or the ineptness of our stories—in many cases he would rule that a story was no story at all. His firm belief was that if the essence of a short story couldn't be conveyed in three sentences, then it was no story at all but, more likely, only a fragment of a novel. We tolerated this principle without believing it for a minute. The whole class, in a semester of trying, never produced anything that Mr. O'Connor considered a story.

He had a problem with me because I had read Smollett. "Jesus, Larry—Smollett!" he said often, to my bewilderment. Smollett he found unnecessary, if not actively pernicious. He was an extremely good critic of the nineteenth-century novel, but showed little interest in the novelists of the eighteenth century. His problem with Smollett may simply have been that he didn't think Scots should write books.

The Stegner class of 1960–61 has now produced some seventy or eighty books. It crops up in memoirs as a kind of star class, though people's memories of it do not always jibe. Malcolm Cowley allowed to an interviewer that I had read all of French literature and had written a thesis on the poetry of the Earl of Rochester. In fact, in 1960 I was still struggling to finish *Madame Bovary* and had never written a word about Rochester.

The value of such seminars as the Stegner class is that, for a few months, they exempt young writers from the solitary effort. Solitary effort, of course, will still be there waiting, but a young writer's ambitions may be strengthened by his being, for a time, amid his peers, in the heat of fervent discussion. Contact with the generation of fathers is good too. I still recall Malcolm Cowley with fondness and value the links he provided to the demigods of *Exile's Return*. It was a good while later that I learned that Hart Crane had run off with Mr. Cowley's wife, not long before he jumped off the boat.

7

☐ WHAT I remember about my first years as a published novelist is how eager publishers were, in those heady days, for new fiction. This may have been because there was no New Journalism yet—once it appeared it dealt fiction a kind of double whammy, since the New Journalists used many of the techniques of fiction while keeping the appeal of fact.

I wanted from the first to write a clear, plain prose but was much afflicted, in the beginning, with lyrical tendencies derived mainly from Agee and Styron. Agee's "Knoxville: Summer, 1915," published in the *Partisan Review* and later used as the prologue to *A Death in the Family,* was a seductive influence, as was *Let Us Now Praise Famous Men* and Styron's *Lie Down in Darkness.* The baroque manner of Agee and the early Styron affected me greatly, but their influence soon collided with that of E. M. Forster, whose prose was much simpler—on the whole a safer guide. However admirably it may have served Milton and Sir Thomas Browne, the high style has never seemed right for the novel—it wearies; it too soon sates the mind and the ear.

I in time came to feel that there ought to be some congruity between prose and landscape. You wouldn't adopt a Faulknerian baroque if your story was to be set on the flat, unbaroque plains of west Texas, as mine had to be, though the dense thickets of Faulkner's prose seemed to me right for a story set in the tangled forests of the South. Hemingway's early concision, in which a minimum of physical description is so precisely applied that the physical comes to stand for the emotional—besides being the most imitated style of the century—wasn't appropriate for my spread-out country. That style soon failed Hemingway himself, leading, as it does, straight into self-parody. Near the end of his life Hemingway was in the hospital with my accident-prone Uncle Johnny, but at the time I had scarcely heard of Hemingway and didn't think to ask Uncle Johnny about the man.

8

⬠ WHILE I was sitting in the Dairy Queen recently, trying to recall what it had been like to start out as a young writer some forty years earlier, I took time out from literary reverie to go have a look at the Fifty-second Annual Archer City Rodeo parade. Fifty-two years previously, as a boy of nine, I had ridden in the first parade. I rode in at least ten such parades, maybe more. In my youth the annual rodeo parade was an occasion of high excitement, but as the Fifty-second Annual passed by my bookshop, it seemed depleted, lumpy, and sad.

In its heyday, in the fifties, the parade would have involved two or three hundred horses, many of them splendidly caparisoned. The majority of these horses would be carrying not cowboys but members of the riding clubs and sheriff's posses from neighboring towns, insurance men and bankers, car dealers and Rotarians, all of them playing cowboy for an afternoon.

For the Fifty-second Annual there were probably only about fifty horses—the one sheriff's posse that presented itself had only ten riders. The showpieces of this parade were the several contestants for Rodeo Queen, all of them looking like mounted JonBenet Ramseys who had somehow escaped the murderous pedophile in order to ride through the streets of Archer City.

There was supposed to be an old-timers' wagon, or at least a few old-timers, but these never showed. It appeared that the old-timers, along with everyone else, had just about had it with the Archer City Rodeo parade.

I watched this parade on the day that the Southern Baptists, in a quixotic spasm, voted to boycott the Disney corporation, which is tantamount to voting to boycott the modern world. It's understandable that some Baptists might want to do that, but if they succeeded they'd starve. It's hard even to get a hamburger nowadays without encountering Quasimodo toys—Quasi to the younger set. It was evident from watching the small, sad parade, which consisted almost entirely of Southern Baptists on horseback, that few paraders had chosen to deny themselves hamburgers, however much it may have galled them that Disney had extended benefits to same-sex partners.

Mainly, though, the parade struck me as being an anthropological recrudescence—the most interesting thing in it was the car Randy Quaid drove in *The Last Picture Show*. Otherwise, the parade was a rite that had lost its meaning and its vitality. No one in it could muster much gaiety, not even the beauty queens, most of whom seemed to fear that if they waved too enthusiastically to the modest crowd their horses might take fright and splatter them over the pavement.

9

☐ LATER SOME of these contestants in the Rodeo Queen pageant took part in that most patronizing of rodeo events, ladies' barrel racing. First, it's always called *ladies'* barrel racing, as if only those whose social credentials were impeccable could be allowed to compete. Low-bred sluts, of which there are usually not a few around rodeos, need not apply. Few rodeo events now bear any reflection to anything that would be done on an actual ranch, but barrel racing, in which a racing cowgirl puts her horse through figure-eight patterns around three barrels, is almost surrealistically pointless, and thus the perfect vehicle for keeping the little ladies of the rodeo securely in their place. *Don't bother me, honey, I've got riding and roping to do—why don't you go ride your horse around those stupid barrels?* It's dressage for the working class—the only people to benefit from this inane sport are the owners of the Western wear stores, who sell the little ladies their fancy sequined duds.

Still, if there have to be rodeos, small-town amateur competition is the kind to watch. The level of skill will be lower, but the fun quotient much higher. Locals who cannot stop fantasizing about being cowboys can give their fantasies life by getting thrown off a bucking horse or maybe by failing to rope a calf. Events survive in small-town rodeo that have long been banished from professional shows: wild-cow milking, for example. In this amusing event a bunch of wild cows are turned loose in the arena—the contestants have to rope them and hold them still long enough to squirt a little milk into a Coke bottle and race with it to the judges' stand. Much comedy often results.

10

⛢ PERHAPS ONE reason I have become increasingly fascinated by history is because I feel that I have had two histories—or, put another way, because two individuals bearing my name have had sequential but largely separate histories.

I was one person up until the morning of December 2, 1991, at which date I had quadruple-bypass surgery at the Johns Hopkins hospital in Baltimore. When I woke up from the operation, after about twelve hours in deep anesthesia, I began—although I didn't realize it immediately—my life as a different person—my life as someone else. I am still struggling, more or less, to reconcile the two histories, to go back to being who I once was, rather than the seriously altered person that I became.

My heart surgery trauma began, properly enough, in farce. About a week before Labor Day in 1991, while driving back to my ranch house in the gathering dusk, I hit a cow. I was rushing home to enjoy the last light from my front porch when a large Holstein milk cow stepped out of a thick patch of shoulder-high Johnsongrass right into the path of the rented Lincoln I was driving. I felt a slight jolt and looked up to discover a Holstein across my windshield, blotting out what was left of the sunlight. Holsteins are not small animals—fortunately this one slid off the other side of the car and walked away.

Having lived in cattle country most of my life, I was not much affected by this collision. I went on home and sat on the porch. The next morning I was coughing and felt crappy. I started to drive to Windthorst and eat a little breakfast when I noticed that the air-bag light was blinking. I had forgotten that I even had an air bag. I had hit a two-thousand-pound cow and it hadn't come out, so why was it blinking now? I called the Lincoln people in Wichita Falls, who said bring it in but bring it slow.

I brought it in but stopped at a clinic along the way to see if my doctor wanted to give me anything for the cough.

Up to that moment I felt as if I had been the sole author of my life, but from the moment my doctor looked and told me I was having a heart attack I felt that my life, for the next several months at least, was being written by my fellow Texan Terry Southern, on one of his more inventive days.

Not being a reader of medical literature, and not being a worrier, either, I was a little vague as to what it actually meant to be having a heart attack. I was hoping to go home and lie down until it passed, but this, of course, was not permitted. Not only could I not go home, I couldn't even step out of the examination room. Though I had driven thirty-five miles expecting to be smothered at any moment by an air bag, a stretcher had to be got into the tiny room so that I could be put on it. The ambulance driver assigned to take me to the hospital—upon learning that he had a semifamous author in his ambulance—freaked out and drove straight off an about-eighteen-inch curb; the bottles that were already pouring fluids into me shook and trembled. I decided at this point that the best thing to do was extract what humor I could from the situation, and there was plenty.

The most Terry Southernish part of the first day was

141

getting to see my own heart on a little four-inch TV screen to which I was hooked via ultrasound. My heart looked rather like a small turtle—it seemed to be pumping along with a will, as it had for the past fifty-five years. Despite its apparent vigor the doctors assured me that I needed more or less immediate bypass surgery—an angiogram had revealed some severe blockages in major arteries. I said "more or less immediate" would have to mean within about six months, when I finished the novel I was in the middle of (*The Evening Star*).

While finishing the book I hied myself to Johns Hopkins, whose doctors were of the same opinion as the doctors in Wichita Falls. However well I might feel at the moment, the logic of the angiogram was that I could drop dead at any time.

I was then faced with a decision that brought common sense into conflict with modern technology. About one hundred years before I had the angiogram, my grandfather had completed his first cabin in Archer County. If there was anything wrong with *him* when he was fifty-five he didn't—couldn't—know it. Common sense, the only guide the pioneer had, suggested that if you didn't feel bad, don't let the doctor cut you open. But the technologies now allow one—indeed, force one—to subvert or second-guess common sense. When I saw my steadily pumping heart via ultrasound I thought that science and common sense were telling me the same thing, but the angiogram—I watched it too—added fateful complications to the story. Tracking a dye as it makes its way through your heart—or doesn't—is hardly a commonsense procedure, yet we live in a time when technology is so confident that such procedures have become ordinary. What would Benjamin's storyteller, the man of experience, make of a technique which allows one literally—not figuratively—to look into one's own heart? The shocks the new, murderous technologies gave the human imagination in the First World War were hardly greater than the shocks the new medical technologies bring to ordinary men and women, every day now, in the modern hospital. How odd to see so clearly into oneself. How odd that anesthesia can eliminate the agony—or at least the conscious knowledge of the agony—caused by the cutting and sawing of an operation so effectively that the patient can never recover much knowledge of what has happened to him. (Since my bypass surgery I've been haunted by the presence of a terrible knowledge that is just out of reach; my brain can't access this pain but my nerves, bone, muscle, tissue keep the fact of it with them, I feel.)

For heart patients, and many others, the spookiest, most Wellsian, most noncommonsensical weapon in the modern operative arsenal is the heart-lung machine. In my own efforts to understand the aftereffects of bypass surgery, now that I've lived with them for eight years, the heart-lung machine figures powerfully and ominously. Of course the bypass operation, as it has been practiced now for more than thirty years, would not be possible without this machine. The heart-lung machine may not really be able to keep *you* there, but it does keep your body viable, breathing for it and circulating its blood.

But the *you* that involved thought and personality, where did *that* go during the five hours or so when the heart-lung machine was taking care of your basic biological functions? Your brain is not dead, but it has been neutralized, keeping only its own secret register of what is going on. The fact that two major involuntary functions, blood circulation and breathing, have been assigned to a machine takes you about as far from common sense as one can go. While the operation is happening you are neither really alive nor truly dead.

Then there are the aftereffects of this noncommonsensical experience—life after such surgery will feel, for many, only somewhat like life. It may also feel somewhat like death—personality death, at least.

In my case the most startling evidence of the profound effects of bypass surgery was that, about two months after the operation, I ceased to be able to read. (The surgery itself was performed at Johns Hopkins, flawlessly.) My recovery had, up to the sixty-day mark, involved no pain and little discomfort. I went to Tucson to get my strength back and was soon hiking in the desert and feeling fine. I had taken with me, to read during my recovery, the little twelve-volume Chatto and Windus edition of Proust, and also the five-volume Hogarth Press edition of Virginia Woolf's diaries: the White Nile and the Blue Nile of language, that is. I read all eighteen volumes with great pleasure, at the rate of about fifty pages a day.

When I came to the end of these two great riverine discharges of words and observations I felt as if my recovery was probably complete, so I went back to my normal life, which involved running bookshops, traveling, lecturing, writing fiction, writing movie scripts, and so forth. But within a few days of leaving Arizona, I realized that my recovery wasn't working. The content of my life, which has been rich, began to drain rapidly away. I had been leading a typical type-A East Coast life, reading three newspapers a day, reading many magazines, and in general, trying to stay informed. But more or less overnight, staying informed ceased to matter to me. Though I subscribed to the *New York Times* in three cities I put it aside one day and didn't read another issue for seven months. From being a living person with a distinct personality I began to feel more or less like an outline of that person—and then even the outline began to fade, erased by what had happened inside. I felt as if I was vanishing—or more accurately, *had* vanished. Thanks to the popularity of *Lonesome Dove* (the miniseries, not the book), I had, about this time, acquired a number of impostors, most of them just middle-aged bullshitters hoping to get a little attention by pretending to be me. During this period I began to feel that I, too, was one of my impostors, doomed to impersonate a person I now no longer was. I became, to myself, more and more like a ghost, or a shadow. What I more and more felt, as the trauma deepened, was that while my body survived, the self that I had once been had lost its life.

At about the time that I ceased to read I began to experience strange night terrors, waking each morning precisely at 3:15 A.M. and staying awake, tense and frightened, until I saw the sunrise, after which, slowly, I would relax and go back to sleep.

The trauma imposed many restrictions. I ceased to travel, except to see my grandson. I was taken in by a friend and her daughter and scarcely left their house for two and a half years. Fiction still came, but it came rapidly and impersonally; my pages were like faxes I received each day from my former self. Many days, after typing my pages, I merely sat on a couch and stared at the mountains, doing nothing at all.

The thing, more than any other, that convinced me I

145

had in some sense died was that I couldn't read. I went to my bookshops but could not connect with the books. Books, magazines, newspapers, review copies, book catalogues arrived, only to be tossed aside. I had read every day of my life since receiving that box of books from Robert Hilburn. It was the stablest of all pleasures, and now it was gone.

The fact was that even then I *could* read professionally: I read seven scholarly books on the Nez Perce, in order to write a film script. But read for pleasure, no. I had floated down the Nile and out to sea.

Now, looking back from a distance of eight years, I realize that even in the first months after the operation, when I thought I was feeling fine, what I was really feeling was relief that I was alive and not in pain. After all, I had had my breastbone sawn in two, my heart put in coolant. I wasn't quite myself, but I hadn't started grieving either, for the self or the personality that had been lost during the process. The violently intrusive nature of that operation—of any operation, really—was bound to dislocate one for a bit, I thought. Car metaphors seemed to apply. I had had some serious engine work done and then been jump-started back into drivability. If there was a little sputtering at first, well, that was only to be expected.

In the fourth month matters worsened—the sense of grief for the lost self was profound. I didn't feel like my old self at all, and had no idea where the old self had gone. But I did know that it, he, me was gone, and that I missed him. I soon came to feel that my self had been left behind, across a border or a canyon. Where exactly was I? The only real sign of the old self was that I could still connect with my grandson, Curtis McMurtry. Otherwise, I felt spectral—the personality that had been mine for fifty-five years was simply no longer there—or if there, it was fragmented, it was dust particles swirling around, only occasionally and briefly cohering. I mourned its loss but soon concluded that gone is gone—I was never really going to recover that sense of wholeness, of the integrity of the self.

That being the case, I began to put a kind of alternate self together, and the alternate self soon acquired a few domestic skills, on the order of loading the dishwasher or taking out the trash. But I still couldn't read. I was at the time owner of perhaps two hundred thousand books and yet I couldn't read.

The problem, I eventually realized, was that reading is a form of looking outward, beyond the self, and that, for a long time, I couldn't do—the protest from inside was too powerful. My inability to externalize seemed to be organ based, as if the organs to which violence had been done were protesting so much that I couldn't attend to anything else. I soon ceased to suppose that I would ever reassemble the whole of my former self, but I could collect enough chunks and pieces to get me by—as I have.

Such surgery, so noncommonsensical, so contradictory to the normal rules of survival, is truly Faustian. You get to live, perhaps as long as you want to, only not as yourself—never as yourself.

Sometime in the third year I slowly regained the power to read. I bought Diana Trilling's *The Beginning of the Journey* and slowly read it through with pleasure. In the fourth year I recovered my interest in the rare-book trade, something that has been a fascination for most of my life. My memory for bibliographical minutiae returned. Once again I could open a copy of *The Sun Also Rises* and turn automatically to page 181, where in the first issue, "stopped" is spelled "stoppped." I began to recall the provenance of books sold long ago, where I found them, where they went when they left my hands. I was cheered to find that a few of my book scout's skills were coming back.

Even now, eight years after the operation, reading is an uneven experience—though I began to read again several years ago, I am only now regaining my velocity—the ability to read several books more or less at the same time, at a fast clip. If many looked-forward-to books fail to engage me I suspect it may be because the operation left me with a less generous level of attention to bestow.

I think of the heart surgery now mostly in metaphors of editing. I am nervous about letting an editor edit my manuscripts—even editors who have known me for years—and yet I let the surgeon, a man I had met for only ten minutes, edit my body on the basis of information from machines. This is not to blame the surgeon, who did a fine job. I merely call attention to the oddity of letting the body be abruptly edited by one who has no knowledge of the self of which the body is but one expression. All the machines can tell the surgeon or cardiologist, after all, is about the defects and flaws of a given body; the machines can't read strengths, particularly not psychic strengths. Longevity is bound to be a chancy thing, a matter of gains and losses, but surely personality and spirit are factors in longevity too. Before the operation, despite my physical flaws, I was whole—something had compensated for the blocked arteries, perhaps for some while and at least long enough for me to finish *The Evening Star.* From the machines' point of view I had been living wrong for a long time, eating what I wanted, exercising only when the mood struck me. Dietary caution is probably the last thing one should look for in an artistically active person. Did Dostoyevsky watch his weight? The artists I have known best never give up anything—sex, rich food, Baby Ruths, Dr Pepper, opium. In choosing the operation I did the correct, the intelligent thing, but it wasn't the passionate thing and I did it without conviction. I came out of it with a sense that we are now, indeed, in Wellsian time, able to leave our basic functions, for quite long stretches, to machines. The question is how long we can hand over these functions without, at the same time, relinquishing our personalities, and our spirits too. The personality might slowly elide until it is no longer recognizable or regainable as itself; it may cease to be the personality that goes with a particular self.

Throughout the whole experience I felt no pain at all in my body, where the intrusion occurred, but a long and complex pain in my spirit. Bypass surgery as I experienced it raises questions that are both haunting and unanswerable. Would I have died, sometime in the last eight years, if I hadn't had the surgery? Would I have lifted one too many pile of books, eaten one too many cheeseburgers, and dropped dead; or would the survival skills my body had obviously already acquired as it dealt with the arterial blockage have been enough to keep me going? I will never know, but I consider it a toss-up.

Most vivid to me still are the two and a half years in which I couldn't read. I would hold a book in my hand but be unable to read it, as if, having lost sight of myself, literature too had become invisible, or at least distant and indistinct. In vanishing, my self took literature with it—and

149

when the fragments of my personality began to cohere again, literature came back with it.

I've related my experience of heart surgery for what help the record might give to those who have this surgery and find that they no longer feel quite themselves. Of course, it needn't be only heart surgery that produces this feeling. Almost any surgery will do it to some degree. The anesthesia itself produces detachment—if it didn't, it wouldn't work. The most passionate natures are sometimes humbled by surgery—quelled by it. Life itself involves a continual leaving behind—of stages, of parts of self. What major surgery produces is a certain quality of loss, a loss with its own nuances, its own character. Proust, had he experienced it, would no doubt have been able to exhaust it as a thing to be described.

The fact that Proust and Virginia Woolf were the last writers I read before losing reading has given them a Delphic weight in my life. I am always flipping through them now, trying to find paragraphs that I remember reading just before reading faded. Sometimes I will seek a passage in Proust that is actually in Virginia Woolf, and vice versa. The two have merged in my memory.

I once heard a famous Washington hostess say of Max Lerner: "Good God . . . I'd rather fuck him than read him!"—an aperçu I've long pondered. She wasn't saying she *wanted* to fuck Max Lerner, merely that, compared to reading him, it would be the less distasteful alternative.

I recall the remark whenever I notice that in the main I'd rather read biographies of writers than read their works. Proust and Virginia Woolf are two exceptions, perhaps because their works are not only rivers of language, they're rivers of gossip too. My time with these two masterpieces I owe to the heart surgery because, without it, I might never have been open to them so profoundly. This is a bonus that goes far toward overshadowing the trauma. My self has more or less knitted itself together again, the trauma has faded, but the grandeur of those books, the White Nile of Proust, the Blue Nile of Virginia Woolf, will be with me all my life.

BOOK SCOUTING

☽ SCOUTING IS a concept that belongs properly to exploration. The scout is one who goes ahead, usually alone, to find the water holes, the grazing, the good river crossings, the game, the hostiles, and so forth. Buffalo Bill thought of himself as a scout, but his claim was not always accepted by his peers. Black Beaver, a Delaware who scouted for Captain Randolph Marcy and, at least once, camped near our own seeping spring, was said to know every creek and river between the Columbia River gorge and the Rio Grande—if so, he did a lot of walking. Most scouts, having only one lifetime to use up, tended to specialize in one locale—at least they did in the American West, once Lewis and Clark completed their epic crossing. The beaver men—John Colter, Jim Bridger, Thomas Fitzpatrick, Jim Beckwourth, and Jedediah Smith—knew the Yellowstone and the upper Missouri River best. The great cattleman Charles Goodnight scouted, when young, around the edges of the Llano Estacado, learning where he could safely go and where he couldn't. In Arizona the contentious Al Seiber knew the desert country well.

Scouts were the freest of men, the most self-reliant, the most competently nomadic—in Africa the scout's boast was that he could walk from the Cape to Cairo equipped only with a pocketknife and a fowling piece.

What the early West was for the heroes of American exploration, New York City, for the one hundred years between 1860 and 1960, was for book scouts—the hunters who scour the shops and stalls of the world looking for un-dervalued books.

Recently I glanced through the 1950 edition of *Clegg's Directory of the World Book Trade* and was not sur-prised to learn that in the mid-years of this century Man-hattan Island had 191 bookshops—and there were many more in the other boroughs. I won't list them all, but I will list those whose names and shops are still most resonant with book people of a certain age. There were the Argosy Book Stores, Barnes and Noble, J. N. Bartfield, Pierre Berés, Brentano's, the Brick Row Bookshop, the Carnegie Bookshop, the Chaucer Head and the Chiswick, Dauber and Pine, Peter Decker, James F. Drake, Philip Duschnes, Edward Eberstadt, the House of El Dieff, the House of Books Ltd, Charles P. Everitt, the Gotham Book Mart, Lath-rop C. Harper, Maurice Inman, H. P. Kraus, Harry A. Levinson, Howard S. Mott, Old Hickory Bookshop, Her-bert Reichner, the Rosenbach Company, William Salloch, Walter Schatzki, Scribner's Bookshop, the Seven Gables Bookshop, Stechert-Hafner Inc., Gabriel Wells, E. Weyhe, and Richard Wormser—and that is only thirty-five shops out of 191, many of which, by today's standards, were more than respectable.

In these great shops were great bookmen and -women. John S. Van, E. Kohn, and Michael Papantonio were at the Seven Gables, David Randall at Scribner's, David Kirchen-baum at the Carnegie Bookshop, H. P. Kraus at H. P. Kraus, Frances Steloff at the Gotham Book Mart, Marguerite Cohn at the House of Books Ltd. Harry Levinson had not yet moved to Beverly Hills, nor Howard Mott to Sheffield, Mass-achusetts. Lew Feldman was at the House of El Dieff, the Eberstadt brothers, masters of Americana, at their shop, and

John Fleming at what had been Rosenbach's grand establishment on Fifty-seventh Street. Downtown still boasted a great many bookshops, including the murky but exciting Dauber and Pine.

Now, less than fifty years later, I'm not sure that New York City contains even one shop of the quality of those listed above, although Kraus and the Gotham and the Argosy and a few other of the older shops remain. There is, to be sure, some new blood, but it would be foolish to claim that it can rival the old blood. The books are still there, in their millions, on the shelves of New Yorkers, but the booksellers who handle what comes off the shelves are far less vigorous and less accomplished than their predecessors.

A time when such riches as those great stores contained were there on open shelves for scouts to study and consider now seems so long ago as to scarcely have existed in historical time at all. I don't think I would believe it if I hadn't seen it. In the whole country there are now less than a dozen bookshops that bear comparison with what New York had in such prodigal abundance, less than a half century ago.

I've always held off writing about book scouting and the world of antiquarian books, even though that activity and that world has absorbed me for more than forty years. What has inhibited me is the knowledge of how difficult it is to communicate the fascination of this pursuit to those who don't share such a fascination. To a book scout the listing, just above, of great bookshops and booksellers is like a roll call of gods and demigods, but to the ordinary reader, the person who cares only for the matter, not the métier, of books, the list will mean nothing.

Virtually the only person who has been able to write about this world with such elegance and good sense that his writings can still be enjoyed by those outside the trade was the English diplomat and bookseller John Carter, author of *The ABC of Book-Collecting*.

In the world of the book scout, reading is only one of the several stations of the cross. A book scout really doesn't need to read anything, except title pages, bibliographies, and book catalogues. A more comprehensive knowledge would not be wasted, and some scouts possess it, but broad knowledge and deep scholarship are to the scout not as important as a passion for the hunt and the energy to keep on hunting, day and night, wherever in the world books may be—and they may be in a great many places indeed.

I'm sure that I've had as much pleasure in the hundreds (or maybe thousands) of bookshops I've been in, going along row by row and shelf by shelf looking for a title or an edition that I've never seen, as my father did culling and inspecting the many cattle herds he bought from. The process of selection, weighing the qualities of various animals, in his mind, was a work that required judgment, sophistication, experience, and—if you will—taste.

And that, essentially, is what I try to bring to the composition of my bookshops: taste, which if applied persistently will result in an interesting mixture of books, none of which is undesirable or unappealing. The iron rule in a bookshop is that good books don't pull bad books up; bad books pull good books down. Even a few bad books can make a whole room full of good books look tatty.

Composing a great or even a near-great bookshop is as exacting a task as composing a novel. One has to be done word by word and sentence by sentence, the other volume by volume and section by section. The travel books, the cookery, the jurisprudence, the angling books require close attention, for these are all categories where dull and unappealing titles exist by the tens of thousands. Having a store full of what booksellers call "interesting books"—their highest accolade—is something every relatively ambitious bookseller strives for. Booksellers who manage, year by year and decade by decade, to keep their shelves filled with interesting books will rarely be the most successful financially. The world, by and large, is well content to buy the conventional standards—the sort of books that make safe gifts to godchildren. But the booksellers who have interesting books will always have the respect of their fellow bookmen. Shops where there are interesting books are the shops where book scouts go to educate themselves.

Ö

MY OWN first visit to a real bookshop, as opposed to the paperback rack at the local drugstore, was to Barber's Bookstore in Fort Worth in March of 1954. I know it was in March because I took time off from a track meet, caught a bus downtown, and visited the bookshop, which is still there, still where it was then, a new bookshop that sold both new and used books. Six years later, while teaching at TCU, I found a very respectable copy of *The Catcher in the Rye* in a pile of junk on their floor. It cost me one dollar and is now worth about three thousand. In 1954 I had never heard of Salinger—indeed, had never heard of 98 percent of the authors whose books were in the second-hand part of Barber's Bookstore.

I had only two dollars to spend, on this my first trip to a real bookshop, and only about thirty minutes in which to make my choice, before heading back to the stadium, where, eventually, I ran a rather slow mile. Not knowing a thing about any of the books on the shelves, I was wholly at a loss, but as time was running out, I grabbed a copy of *Rogue Herries,* by Hugh Walpole. I had never heard of the author but I was looking for something modern and the book looked thoroughly modern to me. I don't think I ever got more than eight or ten pages into *Rogue Herries,* one of several volumes Hugh Walpole was eventually to devote to the Herries family—lesser Forsytes, I believe they were, as Walpole was a lesser Galsworthy—their popularity depending on the then insatiable English appetite for family chronicles, a market supplied later in the century by R. L. Delderfield.*

I would soon go on to buy many books worse in every respect than *Rogue Herries.* In June of that same year, while on a senior trip, I first stepped into old Mr. Clausen's bookshop in Colorado Springs, a shop I was to revisit often for the next twenty-five years. On this first visit I bought a ratty, but to me resplendent, issue of Byron. (The senior trip later became grist: it was ground, cinematically, into three scenes in *The Last Picture Show.*)

Later in the summer, while in Fort Worth with my father selling some yearlings, I rushed to Barber's again and had better luck. I happened onto Ezra Pound's *ABC of Reading* in the New Directions New Classics series; this

---

*In November of 1998 I had a real book scout's epiphany—I *bought* the stock of Barber's Bookstore, and had the pleasure of packing the very shelf where that copy of *Rogue Herries* once had sat.

time, quite by accident, I had stumbled on something that really *was* modern. I read *ABC of Reading* over and over again, taken not only by what Pound said but by the crisp, take-no-prisoners way in which he said it. In Pound I encountered an attitude and a concept of seriousness very different from anything I had known before. I remember thinking, after two or three readings, that this man, Ezra Pound, was as serious about writing as my father was about cattle—in those days I measured all seriousness against my father's attitude about cattle.

In September of that year I moved to Houston and entered Rice. Two days after I got there I took a bus downtown to visit Joe Petty's secondhand-book store. It was my first urban bus ride and my first real experience of black people—there had been none in Archer City. In Mr. Petty's capacious bookstore I bought a novel by Romain Rolland, don't ask me why. I must have been in a French mood that day, because I considered an odd volume of Proust before choosing the Rolland. While I was nosing around in the fiction section I noticed a large crowd building up outside the bookshop—Mr. Petty himself even left his desk to join it. Still undecided between Proust and Rolland, I stepped outside to see what the crowd was about and looked up to see a man on a ledge, fifteen stories up. The man's shirttail was out, a sure sign of desperation in those well-tucked days. Two fat policemen were leaning out of windows on either side of the man, urging him to think it over; but the crowd in the street didn't want him to think it over. They wanted him to jump and were grumpy when, in the end, he didn't. A thunderstorm splattered us, making his ledge slippery: it was enough to send him back in.

A week or two later, after another bus ride, I met the

most elegant bookseller in Houston, the dandyish Ted Brown. Ted had presciently figured out, in the forties, that much of the oil and petrochemical industry was going to end up on the Gulf Coast; the geologists and petrochemists were going to need scientific books, and he proceeded to sell them to them by the thousands. Ted Brown prospered on the scientific books but his heart, all along, was in literature, and he kept a wall—dazzling to me—of sets, first editions, travel literature, press books. The first time I went in I plunked down $7.50, by far the most I had spent on a book up to that time, for a nice early-nineteenth-century edition of *The Anatomy of Melancholy* in three-quarter morocco. I have it still, as unread as it was the day I bought it. Of my twenty thousand books only the Burton and the *ABC of Reading* are still with me from that era.

On my second visit to Brown's Bookshop Ted caught me handling a newly arrived signed limited edition of Faulkner's *The Fable*. "You can't afford that," he said, with a curl of his lip, and he was right. When Ted Brown died, nearly forty years later, I was offered his library, but I was then in the trough of my post-bypass trauma and could not connect with books sufficiently to make a credible bid.

In Houston, as a student, I began serious, almost incessant, book hunting. My searches could not be properly called scouting yet, because it had not occurred to me that I would ever sell any of the books I bought—the Rolland, the Pound, the Burton, and all the others would be my support group once I was back in Archer City, as I still assumed I would be. I began to comb the humbler venues of the city, the molding junk shops, Goodwill stores, antiques shops. Once in a junk shop on Washington Avenue I found twenty-two thousand 78 records, mostly locally recorded rhythm and blues. I was living in one small room at the time—where to put twenty-two thousand records? Lightnin' Hopkins's manager bought them and traveled on them for years.

My book hunting seldom turned up anything of much value, but it kept me in reading matter and also gave me a knowledge of the funkier reaches of Houston that has stayed with me to this day. I came to love the city, particularly its steamy, shoddy, falling-down sections. Houston as a city was a series of crumbling, half-silted-over neighborhoods. You could still come upon little drugstores that looked as if they had been free-framed by a *Life* photographer in the thirties. Once, in a district not far from the slum that's called the Bottoms, I came upon a vast wooden boat, so weedy and overgrown with vines and creepers that it was hard to even guess what period it dated from. It sat in the middle of a large neglected lot, visited only by winos and grackles. Sam Houston could have ridden in that boat, or Cabeza de Vaca.

In the middle of my sophomore year, defeated by the higher mathematics which Rice insisted I master, I transferred to the considerably less cloistered North Texas State Teacher's College, in Denton, which put me within thirty miles of the bookshops of Dallas, a new universe, and one, on the whole, that was fun to explore. Denton had only a college bookstore, but it did have an excellent newsstand, where I bought my first copy of the *Paris Review*—though it was to the more cosmopolitan Commerce Street newsstand in Dallas that I went to secure my copy of the famous second issue of the *Evergreen Review,* the "San Francisco Scene" issue, which contained the first accessible printing of *Howl,* then almost a holy text.

In Dallas there were then three main secondhand-book

shops, representing, respectively, the middle, low-middle, and lower strata of antiquarian bookselling. The Aldredge Bookshop, owned and run by Sawnie Aldredge, a socially well connected, not always friendly man, kept a room full of nice sets and high-end Texana, and several rooms of miscellaneous books. Sawnie bought from and sold to uptown Dallas, such as it was: the notables of Swiss Avenue, Highland Park, and the like. In his shop, just about the time prices for modern first editions really soared, I bought *The Great Gatsby* in dust wrapper for a modest twelve dollars; quite a few years later my partner, Marcia Carter, sold it for enough money to make some much-needed repairs on her back porch, in Georgetown. If we still had that nice *Gatsby* we could now trade it in for a pretty respectable car—a Volvo, maybe.

The largest shop in Dallas at the time belonged to Mr. and Mrs. Lloyd Harper and was situated in Deep Ellum— then a slum, now an arts district. The Harpers, he skinny, she fat, were like characters from Erskine Caldwell, albeit extremely kindly.

The shop that represented the lower depths of antiquarian bookselling was run by old, toothless, filthy Mr. Miles, a character who might have been from Dickens, Gogol, or Dostoyevsky, depending on the day. Mr. Miles's shop was so dark that I could hardly see the books, but when my eyes adjusted sufficiently that I *could* see them, I saw that they were very cheap—so cheap that I once bought forty-two books on one visit and had to lug a vast box to the bus station. In terms of numbers that purchase set a record that stood for several years.

The Harpers' store was vast, cavernous, two-story, with a second given over to back-issue magazines and paperbacks. It was on the Harpers' second floor that I saw my first copy of *transition,* as well as my first (and for a long time, only) copy of the *Little Review.*

This very brief chronicle brings my adventures as a book scout only up to around 1958, when I graduated from North Texas State, began *Horseman, Pass By,* my first novel, and spent my penultimate summer as a cowboy in Archer County. By the time I got back to Rice as a graduate student I had about four hundred books, but had to sell them due to poverty; my second library went the same way, for the same reason, when my son was born in 1962. Somehow I hung on to *ABC of Reading* and *The Anatomy of Melancholy* through it all, but it was good-bye to *Rogue Herries,* Romain Rolland, and a great many other not very readable books. All I could afford during the first years of marriage was Anchor paperbacks, but fortunately, Anchor paperbacks were excellent, and did at least as much to educate me as my teachers could.

From the time I first stepped into Barber's Bookstore in 1954 until only about two hours ago I have been constantly in and out of bookshops—but nothing pales much quicker than a chronicle of books bought and bookshops visited if the reader isn't also a book scout, book dealer, or book collector. I went this far with such a chronicle mainly because I wanted to convey something of the excitement books generated in me then. But enough is enough. Who cares, except myself and his shade, that I didn't buy the signed *Fable* from Ted Brown in 1954? Or that I bought my copy of *Evergreen Review #2* at the Commerce Street newsstand, in Dallas? The contexts of many of my book purchases mean a lot to me, but I doubt that I can expect them to mean much to my readers.

This essay is partly about memory. Why does one re-member one thing vividly and another thing vaguely, if at all? In the course of this piece I've come to realize that the only things I remember as well as I remember certain books, found in certain bookshops, in such and such con-dition, are women, about whom I mean to say little or nothing just at the present time.

If I select a given year, a fairly remote year—maybe 1954—I remember several people with some clarity but I remember the three or four books I bought that year with extreme clarity: the binding, the design, even what part of the store I bought them in.

From the years that followed I can remember quite a few people and quite a few events, but there's no question that I could reel off almost endless lists of books pur-chased, with details about the shops where I found them, bought them, or at least glimpsed them. I have a consecu-tive and continuous memory of my development as a book scout, but for the rest of my life, my memory is full of gaps, and I have to think very hard to get the sequencing right.

Of the books I read at Rice during my first year as a student there, the one that made the most impression on me was Mario Praz's *The Romantic Agony,* a once famous study of Gothicism in English literature. I have no idea why I even picked the book up, but I did pick it up and did read it, and as a result, was soon trying to persuade the puzzled Rice librarians to let me go down in the rare-book room and read *Melmoth the Wanderer,* by the Rev-erend Charles Robert Maturin. Even though I couldn't manage to read *Melmoth,* once I had it in my hand, I was grateful to the librarians for having allowed a callow fresh-man such a privilege. (Later, I briefly owned a copy of

Melmoth that had belonged to H. P. Lovecraft, but I still couldn't read it.)

I suppose what I was doing, in attempting to read the Gothic novelists, the penny dreadfuls, and other forms of sensational fiction, was working my way toward *Anything for Billy,* my parody of the dime novel. I once owned and read *Varney the Vampire,* the most famous penny dreadful, but I never had *Sweeney Todd, the Demon Barber,* a close contender. In a way it was not the texts themselves that I sought, when I sought Gothics and penny dreadfuls— more than anything it was the look of the books, the binding, and the book design, which gave me a feel for the period in which they were published.

Both in my library at home and in my bookshops I have a hard time hewing to any strict philosophy of shelving. Shelving by chronology (Susan Sontag's method) doesn't always work for me. The modest Everyman edition of *The Anglo-Saxon Chronicle* refuses to sit comfortably next to Leonard Baskin's tall *Beowulf,* and exactly the same problem—incompatibility of size—crops up if one shelves alphabetically. Susan Sontag, on a visit when all my books were in the old ranch house, found that she couldn't live even one night with the sloppiness of my shelving. She imposed a hasty chronologizing which held for some years and still holds, in the main.

Susan's principles notwithstanding, I make free with chronologies when the books seem to demand it. My Sterne looks happier beside my Defoe than he looks next to his nearer contemporary Smollett, so *Tristram Shandy* sits next to *Moll Flanders* rather than *Peregrine Pickle.*

Despite a nearly infinite range of possibilities in the matter of book arrangement, I've noticed that most people who really love books find ways of shelving them which respect the books but clearly reflect their own personalities. The historian and scholar Robert Manson Myers had the most impeccably shelved library I have ever seen; he even had an alcove shelved in his Georgian apartment in Washington which held, precisely, his one-thousand-volume collection of the Everyman Library. The polymath Huntington Cairns, who had sixteen thousand books in a vast, smoky old apartment in the same city, held to a rough subject arrangement, with no attempt being made to organize the books within a subject. He had 750 volumes on Plato and Aristotle alone, but was confident that, among them, he could find the book he needed when he required it.

I regret that I never got to see Alice Roosevelt Longworth's many thousands of books on her own shelves— nor did I see those of her husband, Nicholas Longworth, on shelves either, though I bought substantial portions of both libraries. When Mrs. Longworth wanted to dispose of books they were brought down into the garage of her large house off Dupont Circle. They were excellent books, in several languages. Nicholas Longworth's books I examined in a subzero storage facility, where they had been for nearly fifty years. His was a nineteenth-century library, and a good one.

The ability to remember *exactly* where books are is a skill vital to the serious book scout—but it is such a peculiar skill that one suspects it must be genetically determined. Our own shop in Georgetown has been thought to be a very chaos by impatient customers who come in expecting the books to be neatly alphabetized, which, mostly, they aren't. I have long been a disciple of the Dusty Miller school of book shelving. Dusty Miller was a much admired London bookseller, who when asked how he arranged his books, replied that if he bought a short fat book he tried to find a short fat hole.

What this method presupposes is that any real book-man naturally knows where his books are. And not only *his* books but those of his rivals too. The better American book scouts now have a continental grasp of where books are. The late Ike Brussel, a bookman who billed himself as the last of the great scouts, was legendary for the precision of his memory as to where books were in the hundreds of shops he visited. Months after a visit Ike Brussel might call a dealer up and ask if a certain book was still there, third shelf up from the floor, second book from the left.

In my view half the fun of a bookshop is serendipity. I try to compose, first off, walls of books that please and hold the eye—indeed, that hold it so tightly that the eye will desire closer inspection. Sometimes this doesn't work—people will stare at the wall in befuddlement, un-able to discern any pattern. And indeed, the only pattern may be that all the books on the wall are pleasing books.

Other book buyers, though, will step closer, perhaps see a book they have always wanted, grab it, and be led along the shelf or around the room, finding more books and then more books that attract them. A woman who had never been in our shop before walked in one day looking for *Uncle Tom's Cabin* and was led from shelf to shelf until she had so many books piled up that she had to call her banker and get a small loan before she could load them into her car and take them home.

The big difference between book scouting and book-selling and the practice of fiction is that the former are pro-gressive and the latter isn't. One just doesn't go on, as a writer, getting better and better as long as one lives. The artistic endeavor requires too complex a balancing of abilities and energies for that to occur very often.

But the trade in rare or antiquarian books depends on knowledge; the more one knows about books, the better books one is likely to handle—and there is no fixed point, other than death, at which one has to stop increasing one's knowledge about books. This is one reason why the trade is so satisfying—if one has the will to learn, and does keep learning, one will also likely handle better and better books.

Many booksellers live to an advanced age. Frances Steloff (Gotham Book Mart), Bertram Smith (Acres of Books), and David Kirchenbaum (Carnegie Bookshop) all brushed the century mark, and Miss Steloff actually passed it. Very frequently antiquarian booksellers don't even fade—they manage to stay spry to the end. Both Miss Steloff and Mr. Smith could be seen high on ladders, shelving books, long past the age when most of us give up ladder climbing.

The arc of novelists' careers is usually very much shorter, and their efforts bleakly unprogressive. If they keep writing fiction much past sixty, they usually become their own recycling unit, reworking, with less verve, veins already well explored. Self-repetition, if not self-parody, are the traps that await elderly novelists—yet few novelists voluntarily flip the off switch, either because they can't afford to financially or because they simply don't know what else to do with themselves. They grow old, they grow weak, they wear the bottoms of their trousers rolled, but they keep writing.

In book scouting, though, every book read, seen, handled, looked up, studied, remembered adds a grain to the silo of knowledge which is the book scout's main resource. It never has to stop—the silo just keeps filling, it never bursts.

The late Anatole Broyard, who wrote with such enthusiasm about books, was once a secondhand-book seller on Cornelia Street. The late Arthur Cohen was both a good novelist and an interesting bookman—the novelist Paul Auster catalogued for him. The poet Arthur Freeman was for long a director of Bernard Quanitch Ltd, the great English rare-book shop. Many novelists and poets have clerked in bookshops here and there, Norman Rush and David Meltzer for two. But I suspect that I have divided my energies longer between writing and bookselling than any author now working, and the results, I feel, have been wholly beneficial to my writing. The energies used in teaching are very similar to those used in writing; the two professions drain one in the same way, whereas book scouting uses different muscles, requires different skills, and has never drained me at all. Probably my pioneer roots left me ill equipped psychologically to practice a profession—writing—in which one gets up in the morning and then sits right back down, to begin to write.

Book scouting connects directly to one of the oldest motives of all: the quest. There's the quest for the golden fleece, the quest for the Grail, the quest for the pot of gold at the end of the rainbow, the search for the prize Easter egg, the hunt for the rarest books of all, the Gutenberg, the *Bay Psalm Book,* Poe's *Tamerlane* (a new copy of which was found only a few years ago in a book barn in New Hampshire). The book scout fulfills a very old instinct, becomes a hunter-gatherer, searching amid the great herds of books, seeking the next kill.

As with all hunter-gathering, close knowledge of the terrain of the hunt will usually be helpful. Certain books are unlikely to be taken in certain stores. I am fortunate in that, unlike most hunter-gatherers, I have a private hunting preserve: the forty or fifty thousand unsorted books in the receiving room of my own store in Archer City. There's excellent hunting there, and I only have to travel a few blocks to get to it.

The big sorting room is a recent development, however. What book scouting has given me, for forty years of my life, is a world to explore and hunt in, one as rich and various as the great West must have seemed to Lewis and Clark, when they crossed the Mississippi in 1803.

I've bought books in Helsinki, in Naples, in Nice, Edinburgh, Uruguay, and of course, in almost every city or large town in America that has a secondhand-book shop—or even a good paperback exchange. Besides the mental and physical exercise involved, book scouting has given me a world and a way of life to oppose to cowboying or university life. I liked my time in the university, but I always thought of it as a world to pass through. It offered little challenge and not even much eccentricity, certainly nothing to compare to the grand eccentrics to be met in the book scouting world. Scouting, whether for rare books, Coke bottles, or old Levi's, may be the last real home of eccentricity, surpassing, in my opinion, the milder eccentricities to be found in the art world or the film world today.

The rare-book trade itself might be described as successfully cannibalistic. Certain books can circulate around the globe for years, passing from a dealer in Paris to a dealer in London to a dealer in L.A. I once found, in a thrift shop in New Orleans, a copy of John Peale Bishop's *Green Fruit*, his first book. That copy spiraled upward, never leaving the trade, for something like seventeen years, in which time it also spiraled upward in price, from the fifty cents I paid for it to about six hundred dollars today.

In forty years of active hunter-gathering our firm, Booked Up Inc, has owned many, many thousands of interesting books, but at most, only two or three *great* books. The greatest, probably, was an exceptional copy of the first issue of Newton's *Principia* that came from the library of the historian of mathematics James Newman. The second was a complete copy of Goya's great album *Los Desastres de la Guerra,* which arrived so comfortably nestled in a carload of modest art books that we didn't discover that we had it for some months. Great books don't come one's way every day, but they always *might,* which is what keeps the enterprise exciting.

Another curious aspect of the rare-book hunt is how often one *fails* to find books that ought to be there. Henry Adams, when an old man, issued his two masterpieces, *The Education of Henry Adams* and *Mont Saint Michel and Chartres,* in editions of one hundred copies each—he wanted, evidently, to try them out on his friends. He lived in Washington when he did this, and many of the friends he gave the books to also lived in Washington. I spent twenty-five years as a bookseller in Washington expecting to find the Adams books almost every time I went into one of the great homes in Washington—finally, in the twenty-seventh year, my partner, Marcia Carter, *did,* both of them inscribed in a shaky, poststroke hand by Henry Adams.

The migration of books, a fascinating study for a bookman, is usually far more erratic than that of migrating birds. Only yesterday I purchased a copy of an A. E. Coppard book that I had written my name in in 1957, only three years after I had started scouting. Where it had been in the intervening forty-one years I don't know. The clever Chinese collector David Yu told me once that he had lost one volume of Douglas Carruthers's two-volume *Mongolia* while traveling in the Gobi and had reacquired the identical volume he had lost twenty years later from a bookshop on F Street, in Washington.

One reason, I believe, that the vast mass of books about books are so bad is that many booksellers and a great many collectors are only in a special sense literate. It might almost be posited that serious bookselling (like serious writing) forces one to make a choice between reading books and hustling books. The trade literature itself—book catalogues, bibliographies, want lists, newsletters—is so voluminous now that keeping up with it cuts into every dealer's reading time.

Still, the careers of many booksellers, including my own, began with reading. Book scouts—semipros who do not have the aggravations of running an open store—are often very well read. They learn, as I did, that it is possible to buy books they don't want to read and sell them for good money, enough good money to buy the books they *do* want to read. In my early years I looked on bookselling as a handy way to finance my reading, no mean consideration. Two activities that at first seem totally compatible— reading and bookselling—turn out, at a deeper level, to be quite incompatible. The migration of books into a large, active antiquarian bookshop resembles that of the wildebeests across the Serengeti Plain—the books are too many, and they are coming too fast to allow anyone the luxury of reading: it's price, sort, move, shelve, or else be buried in books.

Though it is certainly possible to start low and rise high in the antiquarian book business, it's fair to say that most of the dealers who leave it wealthy came into it wealthy to begin with. Broadly considered, the antiquarian book trade is still a partially avocational, leisure-class profession, the bases of which have never been more brilliantly exposed than in a recent book by the English book scout Driff (or Driffield). The book is called *Not 84 Charing Cross Road,* and is the best corrective possible to the sentimentalities of Helene Hanff. What Driff rightly recognizes is that secondhand-book selling is a once grubby trade that has for a time managed to clothe itself in the increasingly ragged rags of the shabby-genteel. In managing adroitly in being both trade and not trade, it neglected to notice that it was going broke.

Booksellers, when they are operating at the high end of the business, function as literary couturiers, influencing and directing fashions and taste, while at the same time they are also literature's bargain basement, dealing constantly in off-the-rack merchandise. In either case it is literature itself which retains an old power. The little lady *will* just wander in wanting *Anne of Green Gables* for her granddaughter, and she won't want to pay more than three dollars for it either—after all, that's what it cost when she was a girl. Irritating as the little lady might be, without her, bookselling wouldn't long exist—and most dealers, recognizing that, manage to pony up, in metaphor at least, the three-dollar *Anne of Green Gables* that she wants, and will pay for.

Whether they actually read or not, it is the case that a good many booksellers in time become learned, perhaps absorbing knowledge by osmosis from the mere handling of their wares. Whereas teaching tends to narrow in, book-selling forces one outward, ever deeper into the river of lit-erature. Even if the bookseller, pressed for his rent, only has time for a wade now and then in the shallows, he will likely turn up an interesting shell, a fossil whose meaning he may not even glimpse. Years before I had ever heard of Walter Benjamin, I picked up, in the German section of a bookshop in Baltimore, a copy of his *Einbahnstrasse (One Way Street)*. Intrigued by the photographic cover, I bought it, even though I could read only a word or two of Ger-man. I kept it around just to look at and then sold it to an old German gentleman who had been a friend of H. L. Mencken. In a sense that book, which I couldn't read, was the yeast from which this essay has risen. About the time I sold *Einbahnstrasse, Illuminations* was published and I read the "Storyteller" essay while at the Dairy Queen.

Many times a bookseller has handed me a book and asked me if I knew it—in most cases the book will have tal-ismanic significance for the bookseller, one he or she has been particularly moved or excited by. In some cases the talismanic book is probably the only volume in the whole shop that the bookseller has actually read; but like the mendicant artisan or the wandering seaman, he does his duty: he passes it on. It's a modern way of exchanging ex-perience. It was because of David Meltzer, then clerking at the Discovery Bookshop in San Francisco, that I was led to Gershon Legman's brilliant *Love and Death,* and went on to read his fascinating work in folklore and erotic bibliogra-phy.

IN MY time as a bookseller or book scout—the late fifties to the late nineties—what has occurred in the cities of America is comparable to what happened to the mammoths that once roamed the Western plain until Clovis man came along and did them in with his deadly spear points. Once, in every major American city, there was a great dusty mammoth of a bookshop, containing, in most cases, massive accumulations of books gathered over fifty or one hundred years.

In Washington, D.C., there was Loudermilk's, in Philadelphia Leary's, in Seattle Shorey's, in Portland Powell's, in Boston Goodspeed's Milk Street, in Cleveland Kay's, in Cincinnati and Long Beach old Mr. Smith's two Acres of Books, and so on. In that time the many large book barns in New England were stuffed with books. All the cities around the Great Lakes had large bookshops. Some of these old behemoths contained a million books or more.

But then the value of urban real estate began to rise past what could be supported by the sale of secondhand books. Leary's fell, and Loudermilk's—the former contained a copy of the Declaration of Independence that had probably been there for decades, escaping the notice of generations of book scouts. At Loudermilk's, in Washington, a whole floor of books had been roped off for years; when it was opened for the auction the dust was so thick the booksellers had to wear miner's helmets with lights on top in order to collect their lots. There were so many books on that floor that many dealers simply skimmed the cream from their lots and left the rest.

Urban real estate, still rising, has now hunted these great beasts to the brink of extinction, a process that took only a quarter of a century (about the length of time it took the buffalo hunters to eliminate the buffalo). One by one they fell, carried off to smaller dens about the country by dealers who could only afford to take a bite or two from their great flanks. (Marcia Carter and I went in business in D.C. with two thousand books purchased at the Loudermilk sale.)

I lament the passing of those great stores both for myself and for the culture. They were, most obviously, great repositories of knowledge and, of course, were also the best possible training grounds for book scouts, who need to see a great many books if they are to sharpen their skills. It does the fledgling book scouts little good to go into the great emporiums of bookselling—Kraus, perhaps, or, now, the Heritage—or to the boutique booksellers, who will only have a few hundred fashionably selected books, all of them priced to the skies. What the scouts need are the savannas, the Serengetis, places where hundreds of thousands of books crowd together in one place. The second floor of Acres of Books in Cincinnati once contained about two hundred thousand volumes of alphabetized fiction, offering a week's work for a lucky bookseller who happened to be carrying around a fat library contract—but an excitement and a delight even to those who didn't.

As a young excited book scout I would often spend several days in the Acres of Books stores, arriving just when they opened and leaving when they closed. As a book scout I was ecstatic to be in those stores—as a novelist it was somewhat of a mixed blessing. I could pass a whole day just in the corridors of authors whose names began with *C*, another day in the *M*s, and so on. But a sadness would gradually replace my excitement as I worked my way down those hundreds of yards of *C*s, all of whose writers must, when they started out, have had some hope for their books, and yet the sad fact was that no one would ever again read even one-tenth of 1 percent of all those writers whose names began with *C*. I had entered the valley of the mammoths and found what, from a writer's point of view, was the graveyard of literature. Of the two hundred thousand volumes of fiction, at most a few hundred would ever be opened by a human hand again.

But, sobered as I have been by that knowledge and conscious as I am that most of my own fiction will probably end up just as dead, there somewhere in the *M*s with thousands of others, I still loved those great bookshops and modeled the bookshop I am now building in Texas on just such large general bookshops. With a few exceptions—notably Powell's, in Portland—such shops can exist now only in places where the real estate is cheap, places such as Archer City, where, for about what it would cost to park for a month in Beverly Hills, I can have a building that will hold one hundred thousand books.

What I have in Archer City now is a kind of anthology of bookshops past—remnants of twenty-two bookshops now reside there, with, I hope, many more to come. I still believe that books are the fuel of genius. Leaving a million or so in Archer City is as good a legacy as I can think of for that region and indeed for the West.

THE END OF
THE COWBOY—
THE END OF FICTION

I HAVE read a lot of Walter Benjamin since that day in the Dairy Queen in 1980, reading that has left me a little disappointed, even a little melancholy, because I think, by accident, I may have read first the best thing he ever wrote. Of course, what that means is that it was the best thing for me, the essay of all the many he wrote that was most likely to set me thinking. The essay on the storyteller contained a number of provocative comments that I took in just at a moment when I needed to back off from fiction and try to do some thinking of my own: about place, about my life, about literature and my relation to it.

I went on to read pretty much everything of Benjamin's that has been translated. Nothing that he wrote can be totally ignored, for in any paragraph there is apt to be a bright spark of insight, but to read him as a whole is to live a bit too long with disappointment—that is, with Benjamin's disappointment with himself. Almost from the beginning he labored under the curse of the exaggerated expectation which his own early brilliance had created. He is the archetype of the self-disappointed writer, the writer who thinks he should have done more, who lives in the aura of missed achievement—even though what he did write was original and good. The sense that there was a duty to produce a masterwork must have been inescapable for him—he lived, after all, in the era of Victorian-Edwardian-Wilhelminian overproduction—and yet not everyone has the energy for incessant production, or the inclination for it either. One of the ways Benjamin is most interesting is in his resistance to production, his determination, similar to Wittgenstein's, to remain devoted to thought and reflection for their own sake. His was the guilt of the fragmentist, the man who never finishes the great work which he and his admirers think he is capable of. He is all sparks, yet the sparks rarely produce a steady flame; but the sparks do have a white brilliance that in itself is enough. *One Way Street,* his book of aphorisms, is the mode he might always have chosen had he not been seduced by the notion of size, or large ambition, or the masterpiece.

It was not long after his death that Cyril Connolly, another author self-seduced by the notion of size, or the masterpiece, published *Enemies of Promise;* Benjamin himself fell victim to most of the enemies of promise that Connolly so accurately described. What Walter Benjamin ended up with was a few finished and admirable essays, like the one on Goethe that got him noticed so early, and a slag heap of notes, flashes of light that are just that, flashes, illuminations that by their very nature don't accumulate into heavy, definitive texts that Germans produced in such numbers. Someday, perhaps, some critic will take a sharp knife to Benjamin's texts and cut away the many lean fillets of perception from the meaty tissue of the longer and more rambling essays. He was best when composing a kind of critic's notebook, in which he let his intelligence play over what he saw and smelled, whether a new city or a new book.

I suspect I responded so strongly to Benjamin's "Storyteller" essay because it dealt with a mode of discussion that I remembered well: the story orally passed on. Because of when and where I grew up, on the Great Plains just as the herding tradition was beginning to lose its vitality, I have been interested all my life in vanishing breeds. The first thing I wrote that had any value at all was a story about a cattleman's funeral. My interest in the melancholy of those who practice dying crafts has been lifelong and is evident in many books. *The Desert Rose,* for example, was written at a time when there was a shift in taste in Las Vegas, away from the big-bosomed showgirls. Small-breasted dancers came to be preferred, and Harmony, my showgirl, was out of a job, like the cowboys in my other fiction. I've spent much of my writing life dramatizing, in one guise or another, the death of the cowboy, while, in this very essay, I've been writing about the diminishing of the second-hand-book trade, which, if not actually dying, is changing almost beyond recognition. Many of the great rare-book men of my youth—Warren Howell, for example, or Jake Zeitlin—were men who left no successors: when they died their firms died with them.

As for the novel, the form to which I have devoted some forty years of my life, it was first pronounced dead some eighty years before I was born. Even as I began my writing career the death sentence was intoned regularly, many more times. In this case it was a foolish death sentence: there was never any reason why the novel was likely to die, not unless the middle class, which brought it into being and still sustains it, dies first; and there's small likelihood of that happening.

The death of the cowboy as a vital figure has been one of my principal subjects, and yet I'm well aware that killing the *myth* of the cowboy is like trying to kill a snapping turtle: no matter what you do to it, the beast retains a sluggish life. The cowboy has long since been absorbed into the national bloodstream, but is no longer quite so front-and-center in the popular culture. The Marlboro man is a last survival of the Western male in the heroic mode. In Marlboro ads the West is always the mountain West, the high, rich country that runs from Jackson Hole around to Sheridan, Wyoming, where the Queen of England sometimes goes to buy her racehorses. The West of those ads is the familiar, poeticized, pastoral West—the Marlboro men themselves need to do little other than light up. Perhaps they swing their ropes at a herd of horses that are thundering toward a corral.

Horses only, mind you—never cattle. The image of horses running is perhaps the most potent image to come out of the American West: cattle running produce a far less graceful, far less appealing picture. The fact is, cows are hard to poeticize—even longhorns. They tend to seem ugly, stupid, and slow, which they are; images of cows are unlikely to loosen the pocketbooks of smokers in Japan or elsewhere where the Marlboro man and his horses are seen, and they are seen everywhere. No image out of the American West is so ubiquitous, and they are images that are entirely male—Marlboro country is a woman-free zone. Sometimes there is a cabin in the snow, with a wreath of smoke coming out of the chimney. The running horses may be making for this cabin. But if there is a woman in there, cooking for her man, we don't see her: we just see the rugged male, riding the high country forever.

Few cowboys, though, smoke Marlboros. The image is rural but the consumption is mainly urban. One reason for this is that the Marlboro man is so commanding that the dusty, slightly lumpy real-life cowboys don't feel that they can aspire to it. The mere fact that the real cowboys have to wrestle smelly cattle around all day removes them from the world of godlike horsemen. The level of romanticization needed to sustain the Marlboro image is extremely high: it needs the prettiest country in the whole West, plus horses, to keep it working.

Another indicator that the cowboy myth is gradually being absorbed into suburban culture is the current smoothing out of country music. Garth Brooks, who will soon have sold more records than the Beatles, is at the head of this trend. His songs are music for the suburbs and the freeways, songs to be listened to in the cabs of the newer, more expensive pickups; it is genteel music, domestic music as opposed to the loner's music of someone like Hank Williams.

When I look at my list of novels, hanging there like a string of fish in my past, I find it curious—well, *mildly* curious—that I started out, in *Horseman, Pass By*, with the death of the cowboy and ended, in the recent *Lonesome Dove* tetralogy, with his beginnings.

Now that the tetralogy is finished I realize, ruefully, that four novels is a lot to devote to one set of characters, particularly since Call and Gus, as close as I could get to Sancho and the Don, ceased to interest me about halfway through the story. In the first of these books, *Lonesome Dove,* I was spurred on by the thrill of the vernacular, trying to make cowboys speak as they would have spoken in my grandfather's time. In the main, throughout the tetralogy, I was less interested in the cowboys themselves than in the place that formed them: the frontier. I was born only forty-five years after Wounded Knee—half a lifetime—and yet little that I've read since has given a feel for what it was actually like to live on the Great Plains of the West when the Comanches and the Kiowas, the Sioux and the Cheyennes were still free and vital. I've traveled up and down the plains, wondering what the people who settled them really felt about the risks.

Whatever they felt about them, the aspect of the pioneer experience that cannot be overestimated, I should say again, is their land hunger—a hunger of such intensity that it would prompt a man such as my grandfather to leave the settled lands and put himself and his family in reach of the Comanches. To understand this one needs to carry one's imaginings all the way back to the old country, to Europe, and try to gain a feeling for the sense of limits, of being hopelessly locked in, that drove the immigrants to emigrate. With that in mind it's easier to imagine the excitement the trans-Mississippi West must have engendered when it was first opened. None of us today will feel the lure of such a vast, unknown place as the West was then—not on this planet, at least.

What the Western experience has demonstrated perhaps more clearly than any other is the astonishing speed with which things can change. There were so many buffalo—fifty million, by some estimates—that no one could really envision their disappearance, yet it took barely twenty years to eliminate them. Similarly, the cowboys who went north up the plains to the Yellowstone couldn't quite at first imagine that the unfenced purity of the Great Plains would be fenced and cut into ranches in less than half their lifetime. A cowboy of 1866 saw the virgin land as one great expanse, stretching all the way from Mexico to Canada; such a cowboy would have had to be very prescient to imagine that most of that land would be cut up and fenced before he was even middle aged. But many cowboys lived to see that happen, and it left them with a confused, unhappy, bittersweet feeling, unable to forget the paradise they helped destroy. They could never either recover it or forget it. Some may have realized that they themselves were only insignificant pawns in the economic drama of the West. The giants of finance had already begun to look at the West with a hungry eye, and would soon begin to use their might to shape it to the needs of business, a shaping which first required the elimination of both the native people and the buffalo, both of which were occupying what was thought to be good farmland. Though it was easy enough to despoil the West, it turned out to be not so easy to despoil it profitably. For one thing, little people such as my grandparents began to trickle in, settling their sections and quarter sections, getting in the way of more visionary schemes.

I have said that my father studied cattle with the same fascination with which I study books, but now that I've thought back on it, I'm not sure that's true. He studied cattle practically, with a view to herd improvement, or to detect signs of illness in his cattle. What interested him more, on both the intellectual and emotional level, was grass. To the extent that he had a religion, it was grass, a religion whose grandeur and complexity were worthy of him. He was born and lived his whole life on one of the great prairies of the world, on the shore of a sea of grass that stretched northward into Canada, and he retained a religious feeling about grass to the end of his life. He recognized, from walking on it and contemplating it all his life, that the world of grass was multiplex. He envied his neighbor the oilman, rancher, and philanthropist J. S. Bridwell, who had the financial resources to successfully fight the two local enemies of our grass which were the bane of my father's life as a cattleman: mesquite and prickly pear. Mr. Bridwell had the money to bulldoze the mesquite off his land, the result being that his land—separated from ours only by a wire fence—looked like a paradise while ours looked like a hell. Even to the uneducated eye our grass was clearly less robust and less varied than his. The reason was obvious: we had mesquite and he didn't.

Not that we didn't fight it. Whenever a space appeared in a workday unexpectedly, my father would attack the mesquite with spade, axe, grubbing hoe, and kerosene can, pressing a struggle so hopeless that I could never understand why he did it. At best he could only hope to drive the trees back a few yards, and for a short time at that. Within a year or two they would always regain whatever territory he wrested from them. The mesquite was as implacable as the Comanches had been, and far more resilient. My father couldn't hope to win, and he didn't win, but he kept fighting.

I expect I must, in part, have developed my notion of character from watching my father struggle against the mesquite. Character came to mean struggling on in the face of hopeless odds: in that attitude lay the vital stubbornness of the pioneers who refused to acquiesce to the brute circumstances they were faced with daily: the hostile natives, the often unresponsive land, the destructive elements—flood, drought, fire. Some of your children might die, your livestock might starve, the toil to be toiled might be beyond your strength: but at least the land was yours, if you could just hold it. Some could, some couldn't. I think my own sense that nature contained an intrinsic disharmony came from a combination of poultry and mesquite. If nature was the wonderful thing my father believed it to be, how come it was filled with pecking birds and thorny trees? I meant to take care of the poultry, as soon as I got old enough to shoot a .22, but it was clear to me from an early age that the mesquite were there to stay.

My father, I believe, always felt a little hamstrung by his own sense of duty. His brothers left and made modest fortunes in the Panhandle; he stayed home, took care of the old folks, and worked all his life with very limited acreage, which he was only partially able to supplement with leaseholds scattered all over the county. Though historically minded, to a point, he nonetheless romanticized the possibilities that existed to the north when his brothers left home; for all their efforts, none of the nine McMurtry boys got very rich in the cattle business, or any business. They prospered but their prosperity didn't approach that of the legendary Texas rich.

Studies had been available from the 1940s—indeed, from the turn of the century—that showed clearly enough that the range cattle business had never been a particularly good business. It had depended from the first on overgrazing, with the subsequent and almost immediate deterioration of the prairie ecosystems on which it was based. These conclusions were drawn very early and were clearly stated by the Department of Agriculture in its yearly handbooks. But my father didn't like the Department of Agriculture; he saw it as creeping socialism. Studious though he was about the cattle business, he probably didn't read the department's conclusions, which were, in the main, sound. Instead he stayed in debt for fifty-five straight years, attempting to profitably raise the wrong animal—the Hereford cow—on land that had been far better utilized by the animal that had been there to begin with: the buffalo.

Herefords and Angus and other English or continental stock were lazy grazers, and were also ill adapted to severe winters, but the English who began to pour money into the Western cattle business in the second half of the nineteenth century wanted them anyway, and got them; never mind that the cattle died like flies in the high plains blizzards and merely stood around listlessly during the blazing summer.

In a sense the whole range cattle industry, source of a central national myth, was a mistake, based on a superficial understanding of plains environment. As Richard Manning cogently points out in his recent book *Grassland* (1995), 50 million buffalo were replaced by 45 million cattle, to the ultimate detriment of everyone's home on the range. Now the plains are so overgrazed—the public lands particularly—that should a major drought occur, the potential for a new dust bowl is great.

What small cattlemen such as my father got, in place of fortune, was a life that they loved. Seen historically, they were in conflict almost from the first with farming interests. Like most cattlemen my father recognized that running cattle was an indulgence, economically; he would have made more money farming. But it happened that he liked raising cattle and hated farming, though even as a young boy, I often heard him predict that our land would be farmland someday—and farms are lapping at its borders even as I write.

Looking back on the more than forty years during which I have been involved as a writer with the American cowboy, I wonder if part of what kept me interested was the tragedy, the inherent mismating of beast and place, which was always woven into it. The twenty-two years when I was involved with the ranch exposed me regularly to a small but representative group of cowboys and cattlemen—the men we worked with. This little bunch contained all the types that one finds up and down the range country. There were a couple of ranch owners whose holdings were roughly comparable to ours. There were three or four cowhands who were just that, cowhands, men who didn't own an acre of land and never would. These ranch hands were well into middle age; they were not very competent, drew small wages, and lived in single rooms behind the larger ranch houses; their fates were sealed. They had no wives, no visible women.

Then there were two or three extremely competent cowboys who did all the more complicated work; they were smallholders, owning a few cattle, leasing a pasture here and there, which we helped them work. Shared labor is the norm in the cattle country; few ranches can afford to employ all the help they might need. The work exchange is virtually universal.

And then there was a foreman or two, men who managed sizable ranches for absentee (or indolent) owners; the foremen customarily owned no land themselves, though it was the custom for the ranch owners to let them run a few head of cattle, as a bonus for their industry and trustworthiness.

There, in essence, you have the ranching West: smallholders, foremen, top hands, and just hands. Even the more prosperous ranchers were smallholders, really, men with ten or twelve thousand acres, not a vast range in country where it can take thirty-five acres to support a cow.

Occasionally, in this mix, would be an old cowhand such as my guardian, Jesse Brewer, too old to be very active but respected for work done in earlier years and still capable of performing small chores—loading the vaccinating needles, keeping the branding fires stoked, carrying the bucket in which calf fries, mountain oysters (calf testicles), were collected. These old-timers are kept active as long as possible out of a sense of decency, kept a part of the work, because if an old cowboy can't work what would he do but wither and die? So it was with my father. When arthritis and fatigue slowed him to the point where he couldn't move fast enough to get out of the way of a gate or a running animal, the ranchers he had worked with much of his life became reluctant to call him to help them work cattle, for fear he would injure himself; but he had been a highly respected man and they were reluctant to relegate him to an old man's chores. Once it became clear to my father that his neighbors were right—that he was an old man who, for all his skill and experience, would mostly get in the way—he was bitter for a few weeks and then lay down and died.

The tragedy of my father's life effort, and that of many ranchers up and down the West, was that, despite skill and hard work (application, my father called it), they could never really get ahead. At best they held their own, living off credit, struggling, working, seeking a method that would improve their chances. My father read constantly in the literature of the range—the literature, and the science too—hoping to discover some new approach or technique that would allow him to improve his cattle or his land.

The statistical literature on Western ranching, available even when he was a boy, told the story plainly enough. The experts knew early what percentage of Western land had already been ruined. They also knew something about the cycles of Western drought, flood, and winter severity. They knew, in short, that the odds were heavily stacked against the smallholder in the West who was dependent on cattle alone. I don't think my father ever found his way to these statistics—perhaps he didn't want to know them. He wanted very much to make the cowboying life last, and by dint of shrewd planning and very hard work, he did just manage to make it last his lifetime. But tragedy was woven into the effort anyway. He had limited acreage and was raising the wrong animal; he was only able to stay in business because he lived most of his life in an era of cheap credit. Like most smallholders in the West he knew quite well that if a really bad year came—drought or flood—the elements alone might crush him.

I was born in the Depression, only a year after the great dust blizzards that Woody Guthrie sang about. Times got better during World War II, which didn't keep all the people I grew up with from being Depression-haunted. I derived early the sense that solvency was a precarious thing. Now and then I heard talk about so-and-so, who had gone under. I didn't really know what going under meant, but I knew that the prospect of it was never very far from my father's mind, or the minds of his peers in the small-ranch country. People went under, and that, apparently, was the end of them.

From the age of three until I left for college I was sometimes constantly and always frequently on horseback on the land. Day after day I was out there under the sky, a partial nomad, working in fenced country but still much freer spatially than city kids. I spent enough time directly on the land, beneath that sky, to understand that the elements were a lot more powerful than myself, my father, or any of us. I remember riding off in the fall without a coat and watching the temperature drop forty degrees before I could even get back to the house. I remember being trapped on the wrong side of the Little Wichita River when it was in flood, stuck on a weak horse in a world of mud. I was once knocked down by a steer in a lightning storm so intense that the white light made the animal invisible, obliterated by brightness, as if an X ray were coming toward me. I've seen tornadoes just miss our barn, and grass fires come within fifty yards of our house, and yet all these are mild experiences, picnics compared to what the pioneers faced every day.

I've also seen conflicts between men and animals escalate into terrible, Dostoyevskian violence, men beating stubborn cattle with fence posts, fleeing bulls knocking over pickups and even, once, a large cattle truck. All this is unexceptional in Western ranch life. The pecks I objected to from the poultry were nothing compared to the kickings, crushings, gorings that not infrequently occur when men work with animals many times their size.

What struck me in the cattlemen, my father most particularly, was the intensity of their desire to make it last. No Indian ever wanted to call back the buffalo more intensely than the cattlemen wanted to call back the open range. The same land that the Indian longed to see filled with buffalo the cattlemen wanted to see filled with cattle, moving north, though in fact the real open range lasted almost no time. Barbed wire, the invention that was to slice it up, was invented scarcely five years after trail driving began. But in the minds of cattlemen and also in movies, the open range survives still, an Edenic fantasy of carefree nomadism in which cattle are allowed to follow grass wherever grass grows.

The notion that all flesh is grass is one that would have pleased my father; it would, I expect, please all cattlemen, herdsmen, drovers, men who follow grazing animals over the land, seeking the grass that nourishes them. Such men, pantheistic by nature, resolutely reject anything that smacks of the modern world: its politics, its art, its technology. What they accept, at a profound level, is the cycle of nature, in which men and animals alike are born, grow old, and die, to be succeeded by new generations of men and animals. Recycling of this natural sort does not bother men who live on the land; some even resent the fact that modern burial practices retard the process. The notion that they will soon again become part of the food chain doesn't bother them at all.

It is usually when one is in one's sixties that one begins to wonder whether the customary yardsticks by which success is measured have any relevance at all. My father, as he neared the end, counted himself lucky that he had owned a few good horses in his life and had sustained a good name through seventy-six years. Though he enjoyed great respect, and the love of his family, in his last years he often expressed to me his conviction that reality was more than a little cracked. Somehow life hadn't really added up; his works and days hadn't been a harmony, as he supposed they might have been for his brothers and other cattlemen who had accumulated more land and raised better cattle. In the end the two or three good horses seemed to mean more to him than anything he had done with cattle or the range. The winds of futility blew through like northers. What had it all been for?

Cowboys, when questioned, will claim to envy no one—they don't believe there is a more fulfilling life than the life of the range, a life that takes them outside every day to study the land, to work with horses. Yet, in practice, these men are rarely fulfilled, perhaps because of the brutal economics of the business. When I would try to argue against my father's sense of futility he would sometimes cheer up a little, reminding himself that he had his children, he had his good name, and there had been those two or three horses. He could not really hand his children a viable tradition—ranching had by then become an avocation for oilmen, lawyers, insurance men, and other nostalgic city dwellers who wanted, somehow, to make contact with the land again.

Once he was too old to wage war against them, the mesquite soon began to sweep over the old prairie. On the last day of my father's life—I'm told by my son, who was with him—he slowly drove around the hill down at the home place where his parents, William Jefferson and Louisa Francis, had stopped some ninety years before, enticed by water, by that fine seeping spring. The next morning my father lay down in the kitchen and died. The hired man who found him and woke my son merely said, "Jeff's gone."

When I consider my twenty and more books I sometimes feel the same uneasy breeze that my father felt as he contemplated the too meager acres where his own life began and ended. My achievement may be not much different from his; it may consist mainly of the good name I bore and the gifted and responsible son I will pass it on to. I think two or three of my books are good, just as he thought two or three of the many horses that he owned were good. The rest of my writing may well end up in that great City of Dead Words on the old fiction floor of Acres of Books in Cincinnati. I would have liked my fiction to have a little more poise, a little more tact—but those are qualities that seem to have found their way into my son's songs, and that is satisfaction enough.

In my seventh decade I feel a new haste, not to write but to read. The fact of a shortened horizon is stimulating—I feel impatient, curious. I dreamed recently that I was attempting to introduce Norman Mailer to my father at a religious gathering of some sort—of the sort in fact that my father avoided. He must have avoided it this time too, because in my dream the introduction never quite took place. Perhaps the dream came because I had just read Mailer's *The Gospel According to the Son.* I woke with an unhappy sense of a missed chance.

I now think it's likely that a lot of my writing about the cowboy was an attempt to understand my father's essentially tragic take on his own—and human—experience. He was not, day to day, an unhappy man; he was accessible to jollity, joking, dancing, laughter, fun—but still the tragic mien was his and I suspect it was because he saw too clearly the crack, the split, the gully that lay between the possible and the actual. He had attached his heart to a hopeless ideal, a nineteenth-century vision of cowboying and family pastoralism; such an ideal was not totally false, but it had been only briefly realizable. It was an ideal he himself could never realize, but it had been kept alive, though trivialized and cheapened, by the movies and pulp literature. It had even been kept alive by my own writing, about which he had a decided ambivalence, though I believe he had a better opinion of it than his last living brother, Joe McMurtry. Uncle Joe came up to me just after my father's funeral and said in a kindly spirit that he thought I ought to consider going into another line of work, since, in his opinion, I had been going downhill as a writer since my second book.

The sense of that crack in reality between what is and what might be, my father passed on to me; I, in turn, may well have passed it on to James. It may be the crack where books and songs are born.

The frequent presence of my father in my thoughts and memories recently suggests that as we begin our long descent toward the country we won't be back from, our memory seeks to go back to where it started. *In My End Is My Beginning,* the title of a now forgotten book by Maurice Baring, suggests a notion that is itself an important filament in the emotions of older people, even if all it means is that as one is ending it is good and proper to think about one's beginning in order to gain at least a fleeting sense of the whole.

I think I have been somewhat luckier than my father. I did not attach my heart in youth to a circumscribed, unrealizable goal, though that he should do so was perfectly natural for a young man growing up on what was really still a frontier. I early realized that literature was worth whatever it took to attach myself to it, however humbly, and have never had any reason to change that view or regret that choice. I have at times felt the tension between the beauty of the impermanent—prairie sunlight, horses running—and the urge to leave a track. I thought I'd outlast the cowboy, since, as a craft, cowboying was dying when I was young. But an image of the cowboy is still firmly rooted in the national culture, and that has to do not only with the beauty of movement which has been transmitted through the movies, but also with the strength of a life that's linked to the earth. The Western land is mostly not kind—it has always favored strength over beauty. The strength of the land has to be matched by a strength within people, or the people don't survive. The milder, more responsive environments—Virginia, say—might please the eye but seem, in the end, insipid compared to the West.

That I chose to herd words into novel-sized ranches was fortunate. Even if I had wanted to ranch, I didn't have the money it takes. The novel is an inexpensive form: all it takes, financially, to write one is a little rent, a few months' grocery money, and a pencil and paper: one day of production on almost any movie costs more. Although I have made a good living writing, the activity itself, the effort of the imagination, has been mostly untouched by economic considerations. My father was touched every day of his life by the economics of the cattle business, and any moviemaker is touched just as constantly by the need for sustained financing.

I could—and once or twice did—sustain myself by book scouting long enough to write most of my novels, and have money to spare. In the freedom of my pages I have all the possibilities Benjamin's storyteller—whether wandering seaman or village craftsman—would have had. That freedom has been as good a thing as the freedom the first cowboys felt as they rode up the plains at the very beginning of their time, but the cowboys' freedom was almost immediately curtailed by the press of settlement and

the competition from farmers. But my freedom—the freedom to read, to think, to put words on the pages—has
been the same from first to last.

Before sitting down to write this essay I read Walter
Benjamin again. For the English reader there is now a great
deal more to read than there was when I opened *Illuminations* in the Dairy Queen twenty years ago. This time what
he took me back to was not memory, it was Proust;
though, since my surgery, I have never been very far from
Proust, or from Virginia Woolf either, perhaps because
they seem now to have been the last books I read as my old
self; these two great word givers were the end of a way of
reading, for me, and it is to them, frail Marcel and mad Virginia, that I go when I want to recover a sense of who I
was. It may be that who I was was a man with a certain
way of reading.

I have come back a little now—more of that first self
is with me, but while it was gone, I passed from what still
seemed like youth to what is beginning to seem like age. I
read now under autumn's leafage, happily, but with more
of a sense of hurry. I note that George Steiner, in a recent
essay, is annoyed with himself for not having got around to
certain weighty theological studies. Having skirted the
flanks of a few lofty mountains, I know how he feels. I
came from a good father and have produced a good son,
which makes me feel that I have fulfilled my responsibility
to the race. Of mother, wives, lady loves, and *amitiés
amoureuses*—well, that's another book.

I well remember a moment some years ago when I
was given a salutary lesson in the rapid transit of worldly
fame. I was lecturing that day at a small college in Uvalde,
Texas, once home of the redoubtable John Nance Garner,

who as Roosevelt's vice president remarked pithily that the vice presidency wasn't worth a bootful of warm spit. The college was poor. They had never been able to afford to bring a writer in before. The students, culturally, were like baby birds, waiting with their mouths open for any worm I might produce—in tribute to their need I fed them the fattest worms I could pull up. I wanted the college to get its money's worth, and I believe it did.

During a short break in a daylong effort, while back at my motel for a nap, I was informed that *Lonesome Dove* had won the Pulitzer Prize. My informant was my agent, Irving Lazar, living up to his nickname, which was Swifty.

I spoke for nearly eight hours that day. Though it was nice to hear about the prize, a nap would have been awfully nice too. But Irving persisted, determined to communicate to me the majesty of the event. When I finally got him off the line my next call was from the motel office: a reporter and photographer from the local paper were there to get a brief interview and take my picture.

The night before, when I drove into Uvalde, the marquee of the Holiday Inn where I was staying had written on it: "Welcome, Larry McMurtry, Author of *Terms of Endearment*." That had never happened to me before, and it meant more than the vice presidency meant to John Nance Garner.

But time waits for no author, not in Uvalde, anyway. As I walked up to meet the press I glanced at the marquee and saw that it had already been changed. Now it read: "Lunch Special, Catfish: $3.95." Even as Irving Lazar was telling me how great he had made me, my moment had passed. It was a lesson to be remembered. The Pulitzer Prize was well and good, but there was lunch to think of,